HOW TO BE A TEEN MODEL

Jane Claypool Miner

SCHOLASTIC INC.
New York Toronto London Auckland Sydney

ISBN 0-590-32738-0

12 11 10 9 8 7 6 5 4 3   5 6 7 8 9/8

Printed in the U.S.A.   06

HOW TO BE A TEEN MODEL

A Wildfire® Book

WILDFIRE® EXTRAS

You and Your Hair by Elaine Budd
Your 14-Day Total Shape-up by Annette Capone
How To Be a Teen Model by Jane Claypool Miner

Contents

Chapter 1

What's It Really Like?

It is 9:45 on a Tuesday morning in October. Mary Beth Hoey sits in the reception room of photographer Owen Brown's studio. She has come to New York City from her home on Long Island to pose for a cover on a Wildfire romance.

She is wearing saddle shoes, baggy white cotton pants, and a bulky sweater. Beside her is a navy blue garment bag with two formal dresses in it. At her feet is her model's tote bag: a nylon sports bag she uses for her modeling equipment. As she waits, she looks through a *Seventeen* magazine, thinking that her picture will soon appear between its pages. Posing for a jeans ad was her first modeling job. This Wildfire book cover will be her second.

At sixteen, Mary Beth is excited about her new career as a model, but she is also realistic. She knows

1

that modeling is hard work and that the competition is keen. However, she's determined to do the very best she can on this important assignment. A Wildfire book cover will look good in her portfolio of photographs and may bring her other jobs. (The final cover used is on the next page.) If the photographer likes the way she works, he may use her again.

Mary Beth rose at 6:00 this morning to wash her long, light brown hair and blow it dry. After a fast breakfast of toast and eggs, she took a bus to the train station. On the train, she read her English assignment and made notes for the essay she will have to write this evening. It is important not to get behind in her schoolwork because of missed days for modeling assignments. At New York City's Penn Station, she took a taxi to the studio. Now the receipts for her bus, train, and taxi rides are stowed carefully in her tote bag. They are deductible expenses. She is fifteen minutes early for her photo date and is ready to go to work.

No one stared at Mary Beth as she rode the bus and train this morning. Though she is a pretty girl, there is nothing about her appearance that makes her stand out in a crowd. She wears very little makeup and her clothes are casual. Her modeling agency has taught her to avoid being stared at on the street by keeping her appearance simple. Besides that, Mary Beth's looks are the sort that might qualify for the expression "the girl next door."

At exactly 10:00, she is called into the studio by a young woman who is the photographer's assistant. She follows the assistant through a large room with a high ceiling and bright lights. She sees the photographer whom she had met earlier, Owen Brown, talk-

0-590-32369-5 $1.95

WILDFIRE

Homecoming QUEEN

ing to two women. No one speaks to Mary Beth as she follows the assistant to the dressing room.

Inside the smaller room, Mary Beth hangs her garment bag on a rack and takes out the two dresses she's brought for the session. Three women — the Wildfire editor, the photographer's assistant, and the stylist — look at her dresses. Mary Beth sees that there is a white lace dress and an aqua taffeta one already hanging on the rack. She listens as the women discuss the merits of each dress, but she says nothing. That is not part of her job.

Another young woman comes into the room. She introduces herself as Nadia and motions for Mary Beth to sit down. Nadia is the makeup artist and she moves quickly as she unpacks her equipment. Her makeup is soon spread out on a shelf beneath the large mirror. The tin tray of colors looks like a painter's box. There are twelve shades of foundation. A whole row of blushers. Two rows of blues and greens and lavenders for eye colors.

At 10:15, Mary Beth pulls off her sweater and sits down on a stool so that Nadia can begin work. She is a little shy about sitting in a roomful of strangers in her bra but she knows that it is part of the job. Now she must sit quietly but in as relaxed a manner as possible while Nadia paints her face.

The editor warns, "Lightly! Remember, this is a young look."

Nadia nods and smiles as she applies the base foundation with one of her camel's hair brushes. She tells everyone, "I am an artist. Like a painter, you know. Only I work on faces, not canvas."

Mary Beth does not smile. It is much more important to be still than to be polite. She hears all the talk around her, but she does not react. While she is having her makeup put on, she is focused on being as quiet as she can.

She hears talk about the roses she will wear in the photograph. They were supposed to be small and pink. The stylist could only find white ones earlier and now goes out to look for others. The editor and the photographer's assistant are talking about this problem with two newcomers, the art director and the editor's assistant.

It is 11:00 when the makeup is finished. Mary Beth stands and the women all say nice things about how she looks. The art director wonders if she should take off the class ring she wears around her neck. Someone suggests that the ring makes her look like a typical teenager. The editor, who has the final decision, says to take it off. Mary Beth unfastens the ring and drops it into her tote bag.

She is helped into her first costume change. It is a white lace dress. The stylist bought it from Macy's the day before. Someone tells Mary Beth that she will be photographed in this dress and the light blue chiffon she has brought. They will not use the print dress Mary Beth brought because they think it looks too old. Mary Beth smiles because that print formal is her favorite. But she doesn't argue. The client is always right.

At 11:15, the stylist returns, carrying small pink roses in a corsage. She pins them on Mary Beth's collar line, then moves them to her shoulder. Someone else pins a bra strap so it won't show. The editor and her assistant fluff out the sleeves of the dress while Nadia brushes Mary Beth's hair into a soft, full halo. Mary Beth thinks she looks all right, but not that different from when she came in the door.

At 11:25, she leaves the dressing room and goes into the studio, where the photographer looks at her quickly, nodding his head in approval, then turns back to his lights and camera equipment. Mary Beth sits down on a stool in front of a backdrop of light blue cloth. The photographer's technical assistant puts a light meter next to her face and gets a reading. Then he moves to the other side, taking a second and third reading. He reports his findings to the photographer.

Owen Brown is sitting in a director's chair. He has a paper with Mary Beth's name pasted on it in front of him. He will remember her face but needs the paper to remember her name. Too many pretty girls come through his door each week, and it is difficult enough to keep their faces in his mind. He looks at her through the camera lens and then stands up. Going over to Mary Beth, he touches her shoulder and arm lightly to show her how to twist her body.

Mary Beth is sitting on a small stool and leaning her arms on a taller stool. Her body is slightly twisted. The white lace dress is perfectly in place except that it is up over her knees so that she can straddle the base of the stool in front of her. Beneath the glamorous lace dress, her long plaid knee socks look silly, but no one will see them in the photograph. It is only her face and shoulders that will appear on the cover.

Brown takes a Polaroid shot of Mary Beth. The others in the room crowd around the photo and examine it. The editor is worried about the color of the background, but everyone tells her the color will be better in the real photos.

One hour and thirty-five minutes after the shooting date starts, the photographer begins to take the actual photographs. He works quickly, snapping shot after shot as Mary Beth moves slightly for each pose. Someone says, "She's good." Another person agrees, "A natural."

Mary Beth makes no sign that she has heard them. There are nine people in the room and they are all watching her, but for Mary Beth, the only thing of importance in that room is the camera. She smiles, nods, tilts her head, smiles again, turns slightly to the left and then to the right — it is as though she is flirting with the little black box.

At 11:45, Nadia brushes Mary Beth's hair again. There are fans at her feet that have been blowing and fluffing her hair out around her face. For a few shots, her hair is pulled away from one side of her face and left long and flowing on the other side. By 12:05, seventy-five shots have been taken. It is time to change into another costume.

She follows the stylist to the dressing room. This time, she is to wear the bright aqua taffeta dress. They will take only one roll of film because the editor and her assistant do not like this dress. However, it is the stylist's favorite, so they will give it a try. A dress can look different on film. Again, no one asks Mary Beth what she thinks.

Nadia retouches her makeup and brushes her hair out once again. Quickly Mary Beth returns to the studio and assumes her poses. She goes through the whole routine once again. In all of the shots, Mary Beth knows she must look young, wholesome, and happy.

It takes only a few minutes to shoot one roll of thirty shots. By 12:25, she is back in the dressing

7

room. This time, she will wear one of the dresses she brought, a light periwinkle-blue chiffon with a high neckline. Her hair and makeup are touched up quickly and she is back in the spotlight, posing for the camera.

Now Mary Beth moves fluidly, with the ease of a dancer who knows exactly what she is doing. There is an extra grace in her smile, her head tilts. She looks as though she has been modeling all her life. The photographer gives her very few directions, but lets her find her own pace. The tempo of the shoot picks up and everyone seems more relaxed. Around her, the stylist and editors are chatting about the weather, the clothes, and other subjects. Everyone knows this is a good session with few problems.

At 12:50, Mary Beth is led back to the dressing room and is once again dressed in the white lace dress. Since it was everyone's first choice of costume, they have decided to use the last few shots on the fifth roll of film on this dress. Now that Mary Beth is totally warmed up and relaxed, the perfect photo may be found in the combination of her ease and the wonderful white lace.

At 1:00, the shooting is over. Close to two hundred photographs have been taken. Only one will be on the cover of a Wildfire book. The rest will probably never be published. The assistants begin packing up the equipment and turning off lights. Mary Beth goes back to the dressing room to change from the white lace to her own simple sportswear. Nadia pokes an Irish setter who has been sleeping through the whole session with her toe and says, "Get up, lazy dog. It's time for your lunch."

The formals are hung back on the rack. Mary Beth

wraps up the two she brought in her garment bag. She must get her order form for the job signed and be on her way. At the secretary's desk, the forms are signed and she leaves one copy with the photographer. She will keep one of the other copies, and her modeling agency will get the other four. On next Friday, she will be paid for this job by her agency. They will collect from the client at a later date.

Mary Beth feels good about the way the session went, but is slightly tired from all that concentrating on the camera. Actually sitting still for so long doesn't bother her very much because she is in excellent physical shape. She's young, she's athletic. Mary Beth was a cheerleader in junior high and now works out with her school marching band. She also jogs and is on the swim team. Despite her glamorous job, Mary Beth is a very normal girl.

"You know," she says, "you don't feel any prettier. I come into the city and I go to work. It doesn't really change me at all. What I'm basically getting out of it is money. I'll put it toward my college expenses. In a way, I'm in business. Of course, the first year I'll probably spend more than I make, but the next year it should pay off. I spend a lot of money on transportation back and forth to the city.

"I come in twice a week so far. My agency sets up appointments for me to go see photographers and magazine editors. I leave school at 12:15 and have lunch on the train. I'm in the city by 1:15 and making my rounds between 1:00 and 5:00. I catch the 5:47 train home at night. The train costs ten dollars and sometimes I have to take taxis. So you see, I've invested money in this work, so far.

"I like the city a lot but it can get pretty depressing.

Especially being by myself. I eat by myself, and there's a lot of being on your own. But I'm more independent than I used to be. That's good.

"Another thing that's depressing is when you go to see someone and they say that they like your look, that they'll call you. Then they never do. There's no way to sell yourself, you see. It's all in the photos.

"But I love modeling, I really do. It's just that it's not like some people think it is. A lot of girls think it's really so much fun, that you get to keep the clothes you model, and stuff like that. And they think you make a whole lot of money right away. I always thought you made about three hundred dollars a day, but that depends. Sometimes you make a lot less. On this job, I did make three hundred dollars, but the agency takes twenty percent. Of course, on the days I come into the city and go around to see people, I don't make anything. Still, if I keep my young look and work hard, I will make a lot of money for a few years. Of course, the other thing is that I've got to grow some more. I'm sixteen now and five feet seven inches tall. If I don't grow a bit more, I'll have a hard time moving from teen modeling into regular modeling jobs. So you see, I may not be a model very long. We'll see.

"I'm a normal teenager in other ways. My social life hasn't changed at all. I've got the same boyfriend and he's a little jealous about my being in the spotlight. I don't talk about modeling much to him. My friends know about it, of course, but I don't tell a lot of kids at school. I don't want them to think I'm stuck-up or anything. So I guess you could say that modeling's fun but it's not as glamorous as some kids think. It's hard work, too."

10

Chapter 2

Who Are They?

Teenagers who model are many different kinds of people, but all the successful ones understand how to work hard. They get into the business in a variety of ways; the most common one is to send a photograph in to a modeling agency. Once the agency sees the photo, it may ask the person to come in for an interview. There the person may be asked to have other photos taken and be sent out for a few go-sees. But not all models go after the work; some are chosen in other ways.

Mary Beth Hoey became a model in storybook fashion. Here is her experience in her own words. "I was walking down the street with my mother. We were in New York City shopping for clothes. This man came up to us and introduced himself. He gave us his card and asked me if I was a model. He was

11

connected with the Wilhelmina Model Agency and he said, 'It seems like you have the look. Innocent.'

"Before that, some of my friends and relatives had thought I should get into modeling, but I hadn't done anything about it. My mom had been asked to sign with a modeling agency when she was a girl and she never really did it. So when the man approached us, my mom wasn't sure it was a good thing, but she didn't want me to miss out on something she had missed out on. We went to Wilhelmina that day.

"They were nice and seemed to be interested, but we didn't have any pictures, so they couldn't tell if I was photogenic. So they sent me to one of their photographers. She took pictures of me.

"We spent thirty-five dollars for a makeup stylist that day and about a hundred for photos. When the photos went to Wilhelmina, they liked my look and gave me a contract. My mother and father had to sign because I am a minor. I signed in September and my first job was later that month. This Wildfire cover is my second. So I guess I'm doing well for two months. They seem to think so at the agency."

Mary Beth was stopped on the street and was taken by the first agency she applied to. She was very fortunate and she knows it. Other models have worked a longer time to get in the front door.

Tracey Ross is one of the most successful black models in New York City. (She's in the striped shirt in the photo on the next page.) She is twenty-three now, but she started modeling as a teenager. As you hear her story, you will see how her intelligent approach to life has helped her get to the top in a tough, competitive business.

"I've always wanted to be an actress, ever since I

WILDFIRE

0-590-31931-0 $1.95

SENIOR CLASS

was seven years old. In school, I was in plays, and I danced and stuff. I just loved being in high school because I was a varsity cheerleader and always promoting things. Now that I'm modeling, I spend a lot of my money on acting lessons and I also take tap and singing. You see, I know that if you don't have experience, you'd better have training.

"I got into modeling in a funny way, I guess. When I was a junior in high school, *Co-ed* magazine had a cover girl contest. I sent my picture in but it got there too late. Anyway, the editor of the magazine called me and said they'd pay my way to New York if I'd come in to model for them. So I did and they thought I was really good. They called an agency for me and that agency said I should come in as soon as I got out of high school. I was too far away to commute daily.

"During the next year, I modeled several more times, mostly for *Co-ed*. That was before I was with an agency, but I was studying hard on my own. I read every book I could get on the subject of modeling. I'm an avid reader, so that was the natural thing for me to do.

"I was actually nineteen before I went with an agency and started modeling full-time. But I'll say this, girls who go into the business before that need their mothers with them. It's all too much at once for a sixteen-year-old. You can't just turn a fifteen- or sixteen-year-old loose in this city. When you come into this business that young, it's really good to have *mommy* around.

"The biggest thrill for me is the trips. Some models don't like to travel, but I love it. Last December I went with *Woman's Day* to Hawaii. It was so wonderful. I've been all over everywhere at someone else's expense. I love that because I'm a great saver.

"The money is important to me, but I don't spend it fast. People have always told me that I'm down-to-earth, and I guess that's true. I live in New Brunswick, New Jersey, with two other girls. They are students, and when I get home, all of that modeling glamour just washes off of me. Nobody cares if I'm the cover girl on *Ebony* magazine. Of course, they get happy when good things happen to me, but they're not impressed.

"Right now, I'm doing a lot of commercials and that will help me with my next career goal—acting. It's definitely more difficult to be black in this business because there is less work for black models. If advertisers used the proportion of black models to black Americans, I'd guess there would be twice as much work. But I get a lot of work because I'm with a good agency and the agencies take so few black models.

"I get mostly young, junior jobs. I'm all-American. The smile queen. I think that's funny because people think I'm from every part of the world. When I was in Morocco, they were sure I was Moroccan. People ask me if I'm Eurasian. But when the jobs come in, they're for that big, happy smile.

"In my last two years, I'd like to play up my exotic qualities. I'd like to do some high fashion work, if I can. By the time I'm twenty-five or twenty-six, I expect to be out of modeling and into the theater. I've got plans for the future."

Both Mary Beth and Tracey broke into modeling in unusual ways. Most young people take a more direct route to a modeling career; they send their photos to a large modeling agency.

Claudia Black is in charge of the children's division of Ford Models, Inc., in New York City. Part of her work is with young teenagers. She sees the young people whose pictures seem the most promising. Claudia says, "If we opened our doors, all we would do is see kids, so we ask the parents to send in a recent snapshot of their teenager's face. A Polaroid will do, but it should be a straight-on smile. On the back of the photo, put the height, weight, and age of the teen."

Claudia says that she prefers to see girls who are thirteen or fourteen and have a few years of teenage modeling in front of them. If the girl is short, her career will be very limited if she is over sixteen. "We look at the relationship between height and age. Basically, if a girl is sixteen and she's only five feet three, there's nothing I can do for her because in a year or two, she'll have to go into adult modeling. There's a five foot seven minimum on that. The other problem we run into is that some girls look too young. There are some who have baby faces and will always look like twelve-year-olds in makeup."

If the modeling agency is interested in a photo of an applicant, they usually write a letter asking her to come in for an interview. In general, it will only be those girls who live within an hour of a big city who can do teen modeling. Schoolwork comes first. Of course, some girls spend their summers in New York or other large cities, getting a start on their modeling careers. There are other children and teens who live in Manhattan and attend schools for professional children so they can work as much as possible.

Claudia Black of Ford confirms that getting a foot in the modeling door is tough. "We get 175,000 photos a year. That's about fifty letters a day. We also get between twenty-five and fifty phone calls a week. We see about two to five percent of those who contact us. Of that five percent, we take on two percent. And only half of them stay, either because they don't make it, or because they don't want to work that hard."

Modeling as a child or preteen may or may not lead to a modeling career when you are older. Height is such an important requirement for adult work. While five feet seven is the official cutoff statistic, most successful adult models are taller. There are some who are shorter than five feet seven, but not many.

Sarah Duffey is a hard worker who is making it in the modeling business despite her five feet six inches. (Her cover photo appears on the next page.) At eighteen, she's an experienced model who has worn out a lot of shoe leather to get a foothold in this tough, competitive business.

"I really started modeling when I was ten, in Minneapolis. It was a spin-off of the work I was doing in the Children's Theater Company. I did about one ad and one commercial a year in Minneapolis. I first came to New York when I was sixteen, with my mother. Right away, I was on the cover of *Seventeen* magazine.

"That first summer, we came to New York for three weeks and then we went home for three weeks. Then we came back for the next three weeks. The next summer, we were here longer. I would guess that my mother and I spent about six thousand dollars more than I made those first two summers. That's a very big investment, but we had discussed

17

it carefully. My dad said it would be like my college education.

"I came to New York by myself after I graduated from high school. I made a little money but nothing big. Then I went home and I was thinking about going to college. I knew how tough it would be to make it in modeling at my height, and I was homesick. However, I ended up going to Italy instead and that was a big boost to my career.

"A lot of models go to Europe because it is easier to break in there. Going to Europe is really good for your portfolio and sometimes the agency advances money for your plane ticket and hotels. But I did it all on my own because I like to be independent.

"I met this man who was with an Italian agency and he said I'd do really well. He was right, because I was on several covers over there. The best part about it was that I was able to live with my aunt and uncle, who have a house in Milan. I am so lucky.

"I've been in New York for three months now and I'm working very hard. There's been a cover for *Young Miss* magazine, a Maybelline ad, and several catalog jobs. I'm doing very well for my height.

"Financially I'm still in the hole, but I'm making it. I room with two girls — one dancer and one singer. I work in an ice-cream shop several nights a week and that helps. Most of my work is teen work because I'm young-looking for eighteen. I hope to model for a few more years and save some money.

"I have two possible careers after that. I'd like to have a career in acting but it all depends. I've done some television commercials in Italy and Minnesota but none in New York as yet. I had a nice audition today and I felt good about it. Commercials could help me with my acting goal.

"The other career possibility for me would be dermatology. If I save enough money for medical school, that will be great. At any rate, I'm realistic about my modeling career. It won't last forever, even if I make it big."

One very successful male model who is with the Ford Agency started as an actor when he was a teenager. Now he does many television commercials as well as print modeling jobs. At twenty-three, Howard Balaban thinks of himself as an old-timer in the business. (His cover shot appears on the next page.)

"I started getting paid for acting and modeling at age fifteen. Before that, I'd done a lot of acting in school. I was a big hit in junior high when I played Tevye in *Fiddler on the Roof*. You see, I really loved acting from the minute I got into it.

"When I went to high school, I got a job as an actor in the Huntington Valley Dinner Theater. I made a hundred and twenty dollars a week. Somebody in the cast told me I could make sixty dollars an hour as a model, so I decided to try that. That was when I was fifteen, but I was already close to six feet tall, which is what you have to be to be a male model.

"I had this guy take my first pictures. Then I went down to the second largest agency in Philadelphia and showed them my pictures. The guy there said that I would never make it as a model. That didn't discourage me as much as you might think. The next week, I went to the biggest agency in Philadelphia and there was no one in the office except the boss — Paul Midiri. He told me to come in, and he signed me

WILDFIRE

JUST
Sixteen

TERRY MORRIS

up the same day. Then he sent me out on a go-see for a big navy training film. I was scared to death but I went down there and two weeks later I got a call for the part. I made ten thousand dollars on my first job.

"I worked all the rest of the way through high school in Philadelphia. When I graduated, I came to New York. The truth is, I didn't like New York very much and I wasn't sure I wanted to make the change, but I knew that was where the big money was.

"When I came to New York four years ago, there weren't too many guys in town who had that young look. So I made it at just the right time. For me, modeling is a business just like any other kind of selling. Only you're selling yourself.

"New York City was a big shock. I was kind of lost for two years. To show you what I mean, I moved seven different times, just going from sublet to sublet. But it was good I came here so young because I learned a lot. You learn how to take care of yourself. That's one thing. I found out fast that the guys who were smart were running a good business and making it. I came here with guys who were just as good-looking as I was but they didn't make it because they weren't out working the streets and being salesmen. I did a lot of footwork and I was pushy.

"As a teenager, I wasn't going to make it in the high fashion market. I did a lot of catalog work — J.C. Penneys, Sears, young commercials, running and jumping, things like that. I did Close-Up toothpaste commercials and things like going into the candy store with Dad. I still do teen work, but I'm beginning to get grown-up things, too.

"Also, my acting is coming along. I've been studying for three years and I've screen-tested fifteen times. ABC just flew me out to do a live thing for them. Right now, my age makes it hard for me to find acting work. I either have to be the star or there's no job. But eventually, I plan to get into film production. That's the reason I want the acting, so I can get into the other side of the business.

"I would say that for a guy with the look, New York City can be the hottest town in the world — if he has the guts and knowledge and knows how to sell himself. But it takes a *lot* of guts. In any business, there's a lot of rejection, and in this business, there's even more. So you have to be prepared for that to make it."

Lynea Forseth's photographs are typical *all-American* or *sunny California* girl. She looks young, innocent, and happy, and that is exactly the way she talks as she describes her work as a teenage model.

"I'm sixteen now and I've been modeling for a year and a half. I love it, and so far I've had fantastic experiences. Even the way I got into modeling was a terrific adventure.

"It was just incredible how it happened. My father is a pastor in a church on Long Island and we were having this church event. A man I didn't know kept following me around and I was getting kind of nervous. When he came up to me and said I should be a model, you can guess what I thought!

"But he got me an interview with some people at *Seventeen* magazine and I went to see them. It was incredible, I guess, but they said they had a job for me the next week. I posed for the Japanese edition of *Seventeen* magazine. Then they said they had another job for me with the American *Seventeen*. Also, they called a modeling agency for me and I signed up. I started doing commercials right away. I've also done covers for several teenage romances. I am on the cover of *Senior Class* (Wildfire) with Tracey Ross. (See page 13.)

"The biggest obstacle I've faced was making the decision to become a model. My father had a lot of reservations about it because he is a pastor and his congregation is fairly conservative. But that has worked out very well. I even had a story printed about me in *Winner's Circle*, which is a religious magazine.

"The other consideration was that I'd always had my heart set on being a pediatrician and I want to go to college. But I have four brothers, and the money I make from modeling will be great. So in some part, my decision to try modeling was financial.

"I'm still in high school, but I'm combining my eleventh and twelfth grades so I can move to the city next year. I'll go to New York University and continue modeling. With my young look, I should be doing teen modeling for quite a while — at least, I hope so.

"Right now, I come into the city four times a week. My mother drives me when she can, but she's in college herself so at least one or two times a week, I take the train in by myself.

"My first year, I was doing a lot of editorial work, which doesn't pay as well so I just broke even. Now I'm getting a lot of commercials and that really pays well. I love doing them because I've always been interested in acting, though I haven't had a chance to be in school plays or anything. I did go in for competition figure skating, and I still keep that up but not as much as I used to.

"One of the best things about modeling has been getting to know other girls. I've spent the night in New York with friends several times and that's great. Most of the girls I've met are really wonderful.

"Of course, there are a lot of different personalities, and I think some feel the competition and strain. That's something you have to be able to deal with. You have to be able to handle rejection. I see things that are wrong with my features and stuff like that, but I'm my own person and so I try not to compare myself with anyone else. Most of my jobs are for teens who are about sixteen but I go down to thirteen or fourteen.

"I think modeling has given me poise in every area. I went for an interview at New York University for college application and it felt very easy. That's because of all the go-sees I've done.

"I'll probably continue as a model all the way through college. If I'm at NYU, I can work part-time and my agency is happy with that because most teen work is in the afternoons, anyway. I'm a 3.8 student in high school and the modeling hasn't hurt my grades. Eventually, I see my future in medicine.

"My biggest thrill? That was the first photograph, of course. I remember running into the drugstore and grabbing the magazine. I just sat there about fifteen minutes looking at myself. You fantasize about it but you don't think it could really happen to you."

As you can see, teenage models come from many different backgrounds and approach their work in different ways. For some, like top model Jayne Mo-

I'm Christy

WILDFIRE

MAUD JOHNSON

dean, it seems as easy and pleasant as a fairy tale. (See her cover on the opposite page.) For others, there is a long period of work before the glamorous life begins. But whether the beginning is accidental or a difficult and slow process, no one stays at the top very long without hard work and good habits. The life of the teenage model is a life of dedication and discipline.

Chapter 3

What Kind of Work?

Not all modeling work is for print or television, though those are the jobs that most young people dream about. While it is certainly true that television commercials and photographic dates pay the largest fees, there are many other ways to earn money as a model.

Perhaps ninety percent of all modeling jobs are in fashion. Not only do all the major designers and manufacturers of clothing hire models, but so do many department and specialty stores.

Runway modeling is probably the best known of the nonphotographic kinds of modeling. Some of the top models of the world work for important design houses as runway models. The pay for the most professional can compete with the fees that the print models earn.

Runway models must be at least five foot eight and not more than five foot ten inches tall. They must fit a size six or eight perfectly. While they need not be photogenic, their appearance must be very attractive. Excellent figure, good teeth, clear skin, and healthy hair are absolute musts. One of the most important parts of being a runway model is being able to move with grace and vitality.

In runway modeling, there is room for many different types of beauty. Some sportswear designers will want girls who appear young and carefree, while the high fashion designers may look for an exotic or glamorous sleekness. Often the runway model will be required to wear many different types of costumes and change her appearance accordingly.

Learning to walk on a runway is the most important step toward this type of modeling. The second step is learning to change clothes quickly and adapt your appearance to the costume. Many runway models learn to control and change their hairstyles very quickly.

Since runway walking consists of turning quickly and moving in such a way as to show off the best qualities of a costume, many runway models spend a lot of time exercising. Yoga, dance, or other exercise will help body flexibility and add grace to the model's movements.

Many teenagers find that runway modeling is a good way to begin a career. Especially in small towns, fashion shows may be the easiest kinds of modeling jobs to obtain. Diane Westbury, who is now a top New York City model, began her career at age fifteen in her hometown of St. George, South Carolina. She modeled for boutiques and department stores until she'd developed enough experience to try the Big Apple. She is quoted in the June, 1979, issue of *Seventeen* magazine as saying, "The firsthand experience I got at home really prepared me."

Only the top designers and department stores pay their runway models large fees. Often, the jobs available to teenagers in small towns will pay as little as five dollars an hour. However, the experience gained in runway modeling is very important since the runway model must learn to move quickly and not make any mistakes. While the print model can pose for as many as two hundred photos in one sitting and have only one printed, the runway model has no room for error. She gets only one chance to walk out onto that stage and show her costume to its best advantage.

Showroom modeling is similar to runway modeling because the clothes are shown to customers on live people. However, most runway modeling is aimed at women who will be wearing the clothing, and most showroom modeling is aimed at buyers who will purchase large amounts of clothing for their stores. A showroom model works for the manufacturer of the clothing. Often she is on salary and works five days a week. Sometimes she is asked to do office work or sales in addition to modeling clothes.

The requirements for showroom modeling are slightly different than for print or runway modeling. You must have a good figure and be able to show off the clothing. You must also be able to change quickly and walk gracefully. Just as important as these skills is your ability to talk effectively to customers. Often, the showroom model is expected to explain fabrics and quote prices and code numbers as she shows the garments. A good personality and lots of poise are very important to the showroom model.

Usually showroom modeling jobs are for older models who are able to work full-time. While a teenager who lives near designers or manufacturers might find some part-time work during the busy season, most of these jobs will have to be approached after graduation from school. The best preparation for showroom modeling is experience in runway modeling and knowledge of fashion and fabrics. The jobs will particularly appeal to young women who are interested in job security or in eventually having careers in fashion merchandising.

Some department stores hire models to show clothes to customers. Usually these models work in the most expensive departments of the stores. The jobs combine some of the aspects of showroom and runway modeling. Usually they are available to older models, since most teen fashions are not expensive enough to merit this sort of presentation.

Other department-store modeling jobs are available to teen models. There are the fashion shows, of course. Besides those organized activities, department stores often hire part-time models to demonstrate cosmetics or clothing on an informal basis.

Informal modeling in stores is probably the easiest kind of modeling work to obtain. Sometimes girls are hired as salespeople and asked to model clothes while they work. That kind of modeling really means nothing more than selecting an outfit in the morning and wearing it during the day. On some jobs, the salesperson might be asked to change two or three times a day or even every hour. While not strictly modeling jobs, these sales positions are good experience for would-be models.

Sometimes pretty girls are hired as models for trade shows or conventions. As a rule, the girls are not selling clothes. Rather, they are hired to attract attention to other products. For instance, you will often see attractive young women in flashy costumes standing beside trailers or automobiles during an automobile trade show. Sometimes the young women are asked to distribute leaflets or brochures for products that can range from tractors to fountain pens.

Passing out leaflets at a convention for automobile distributors is very different from posing for the cover of *Vogue* magazine, yet both jobs are called modeling. Most of the part-time jobs in fashion shows or at conventions pay less. You might make between five dollars an hour and two hundred dollars a day, depending on your experience and the type of job. But whether the pay is large or small, the requirements for the job are high and the competition is keen. Any sort of modeling work attracts applicants.

Chapter 4

What Does an Agency Do?

There are about 70,000 part-time or full-time modeling positions in the United States, and the best way to find the good jobs is to register with a modeling agency. Especially if you are hoping for a career in print or television, you will want an agency affiliation. Nearly all the photographic assignments and even more of the television jobs come through agencies.

Though you have read about some models who got one or two jobs before they registered with an agency, it is just about impossible to do very much print work if you are independent. Photographers call the agencies and tell them what sort of look they need. It is the agency that sends the girls out for go-sees. Most photographers would assume that any really good model would be with an agency.

Jobs that require runway work are also often filled by agencies. Most department stores regularly use agencies to find the models for their fashion shows. Only the lowest salaried jobs or those that are part-time sales jobs will not want an agency connection.

Because so much of the work is filled by agencies, anyone who is serious about a modeling career will first try to locate a legitimate agency. The search for the right agency can be time consuming, but it will pay off. The right agency can mean the difference between success and failure.

Many of the best and biggest modeling agencies are in New York City. That's because so much television and print work is done in Manhattan. It is natural that the biggest names such as Elite, Ford, Legends, Prestige, Wilhelmina, and Zoli are all located there.

Such agencies are contacted for the highest paying jobs available, and all the top models in the United States are registered with one of them. Some of their models make a thousand dollars a day or more. These are the top agencies, but there are many other reputable agencies in New York City and other large cities. Chicago, Dallas, Los Angeles, and Miami have plenty of modeling opportunities for a girl to make money in the print and television business. Smaller cities probably offer more print and fashion work than television, but they can be great places for modeling careers.

Some agencies specialize in certain types of models. Marge McDermott in New York City is a top agency for children and young teens. An agency called Funny Face specializes in people who are not beautiful but have interesting, attractive, and arresting appearances. Often the people used in television commercials look more like the girl or boy next door than the unattainable beauty. Some of these people are called "characters" or "real people." There are also agencies that specialize in heavier models and others that have only black or Oriental models.

Since the best-known agencies have their pick of the young women who want to be models, some girls are tempted to apply to the less well-known agencies first. Professionals in the business say that's not always a good idea. One woman who works for a top agency had this to say: "We need new faces and we're always on the lookout. But more than that, we may be more willing to experiment a bit, to take a chance on the girl with an arresting face rather than just classical good looks."

Most models are aware that their features have bad as well as good points. They learn to present the most attractive aspects of themselves to the public. Young women who want to be models may be comparing their appearances to the finished photographs in magazines, forgetting that there were as many as two hundred other photographs that were probably not as good. "Aim for the top," one high-earning model urged. "You won't really know until you try whether or not you've got the look."

Approaching a modeling agency can be very frightening. Louise Roberts, vice president of Prestige Models, has this to say about that first interview: "They come in and they all look pretty, but sometimes that's not enough. The typical girl is one who has heard all her life that she's beautiful enough to be a model. She comes in and she's scared. I try to put her at ease and to tell her the truth as I see it. Noses and upper lips are tough spots. Sometimes a girl can be very pretty but just not have the bone structure. I look for a girl with what I call the 'x factor.' She has to have that certain something that will light up the room. We can clear up her skin, put her on a diet, or have her teeth fixed, but she has to have that special magic when she walks in the door."

How can a young woman tell if she is the one in a thousand who has that x factor? Often there is no way to tell without approaching the best agencies and getting their opinions. Tracey Ross, Wilhelmina model, has this advice for beginners: "Don't wait until you think everything about you is perfect. Some girls think they have to lose another five pounds. With me, I wanted all my fingernails to be exactly the same length. Talk about nitpicking! The truth was, I was scared. But I would say to you, any girl who has it in her mind to be a model should just go ahead and try. Jump right in. Go ahead and try for the top. I did and I'm glad."

Approaching an agency can be done several ways. The most common is to send your photograph and measurements with a letter asking if you can come in for an interview. In the letter, be sure to state how old you are and how much longer you will be in school. Tell them whether or not you live close enough to model after school. Generally agencies will consider part-time work agreements for young people who live within an hour and a half of them. Young people who live farther away might agree to work only during the summer.

Many girls worry a lot about the photograph that they send in to the agency. They can spend a lot of money for professional photographs. Again, Tracey Ross has good advice for the beginner. "I think too many girls get the best photographer in, say, Oshkosh, and spend three hundred and fifty dollars shooting with somebody who if he were any good would be in the big city. Putting together portfolios of photos is a big, organized rip-off and girls should be careful. Save your money."

She goes on, "Even if an agency likes a girl, they'll take her whole book of pictures and throw it in the trash. They don't salvage one because they work with the best photographers in the world. So I would say to girls, get a head shot, a bathing-suit shot, and a fashion shot at most. You can do with a lot less.

"The photograph that got me my first modeling job was taken in the kitchen by my mother. If somebody's got a thirty-five millimeter camera, here is something you can keep doing: Whenever you think you look particularly good, have your friend take your picture. Pose in different ways. Experiment with makeup. You can even take your own picture if your arms are long enough. They will just see your face. If you shoot five rolls of film, you're bound to get a good shot or two. Besides, that's the way to see your own flaws.

"Every time you get some pictures developed, study them. See that you've got to stop wearing your hair like that. Or use your eye shadow differently. When you get a good photo, blow it up. Take the ones that you think look like you at your best."

You can find the names of the modeling agencies in your area in the Yellow Pages of the telephone book of the city nearest you. Public libraries usually have telephone books for those cities if they are out of your own area. Or you may have to make a trip to the city to copy all of the names down.

Going in to see a representative at an agency may be easy or difficult to arrange, depending on the agency policy.

"We just don't have time to see them all," one executive explains. "The initial photograph screens out the impossible ones. If I opened my door to every little girl whose mother thinks she should be a model, I'd never get anything else done."

On the other hand, some of the top agencies in the world see everyone who comes to the door. Often they have a special hour of the day or special day of the week when they interview applicants. You want to be sure to arrive at the proper time so that you don't waste their time or your own.

Expect the interview to be very short. The person in charge will ask you a few questions about yourself: your age, your hometown, your experience, and when you would be available to work. Then she will look at your photographs and thank you for coming in. When you understand that they take only a small percentage of the young women who come in the door, you realize that rejection is nothing to be ashamed of.

"Some girls burst into tears," Louise Roberts of Prestige says. "But I have to tell them the truth. Of course, I always add that that is only my opinion. Some other agency may take them on."

Handling rejection is a very big task in the modeling business, and some girls find in their initial interviews that modeling will never be for them. One successful minister confessed, "I went out on a lot of modeling interviews when I was a teenager, but I couldn't stand the rejection. They would look me over and then send me away. Once or twice, when I got jobs, I felt just about as bad. Who you were simply didn't matter. All they cared about was how you looked. So I gave it up and went back to college and I'm very glad I did."

Modeling agency executives are aware of the strain that modeling can put on teenagers. The legitimate agencies try very hard to protect and help their young workers. Dan Deeley of Wilhelmina says, "When you're dealing with young people, you can't just leave them up to the fates. You keep a real close eye on teenagers. We act as second parents."

Finding a good agency is the first step in a modeling career, and it can sometimes be very difficult. If the town closest to where you live has only one agency and it turns you down, you may feel stumped. Sometimes young women delay their careers until they are out of high school and can go to larger cities.

What if you send your photograph or visit many different agencies and they all turn you down? What should you do then? Sarah Duffey, Ford model, has this advice for beginners: "Be sure to try all the agencies before you give up. But listen to what they say, because you have to be realistic. Sometimes we don't know what we really look like. If you've been turned down by them all and you think they're wrong, go home and work on it some more. Come back and try again. I'd say if they still turn you down it is time to start thinking about another career."

Claudia Black, director of the children's division at Ford, echoes Sarah Duffey's advice. "There's nothing wrong with trying, but if you've gone to every agency and they've all said no, then be realistic and say this isn't for me."

However, Claudia points out that teens often change a great deal as they grow older, and that can be an important factor. "Girls will change. Some go through ugly-duckling stages. So if you change drastically between, say, fourteen and eighteen, try once again. It's important to know when not to give up. If you look like the girls you see in magazines, give it a try. After you've been rejected by every agency, don't waste your time worrying about it. Go on to something else you're interested in."

Modeling agencies cannot afford to take on a girl who they are sure will not get work. Since agencies have a large investment in the girl's training and photographs, and since they sometimes advance money for transportation and other expenses, they are very careful about their choices. Legitimate agencies *never* charge girls to register with them. They earn their money from the commissions their models pay after they get modeling work.

If an agency asks you for money to get you jobs, walk the other way. They probably can't get you good jobs or they wouldn't have to make their money off your registration fees. If you are confused by their statements and not sure whether or not they are honest, you might check with your state Consumer Protection Agency or the Better Business Bureau closest to you. Be very careful before you sign anything. A dishonest agency won't do you any good. Don't be tempted by their promises, no matter how great.

Another common way that young people are cheated is by paying large amounts of money to photographers who promise great things as a result of their work. Successful fashion photographers earn their money from clients who pay to have their product advertised. If they ask models for money, they must not be very successful at their work and probably will not be able to help you.

As you have read, young people are sometimes contacted by agencies in unusual ways. A representative of an agency might stop you on the street and ask you to come in and talk with them. Someone you meet socially might tell you that you would be a good model and arrange for you to meet someone he or she knows who works for a magazine or modeling agency. These things do happen, especially if you live in a big city like New York.

"We have stopped people on the street," Dan Deeley, director of the men's division of Wilhelmina Model Agency, says. "We have seen pictures of someone who is a relative of someone. We see photos of contest winners, that sort of thing. A lot of referrals come in from models who are already working with us. A model of ours, Wendy Rossmeyer, brought in a photo of someone she'd grown up with. That's how we got Kevin Honan, and we're very excited about him. He's brand, brand-new and we think he's going to do very well."

Of course, you must be very careful about these sorts of contacts. Any legitimate person who works for a modeling agency will have a business card. He or she will want you to come to an agency at a later date with your parent or guardian. *Never* go with someone who promises you a modeling job that very minute. That is not the way the business works and it could be dangerous.

A legitimate agency will expect to work with your parents as well as with you, since minors cannot make legal contracts. It is quite usual for parents to attend the first few visits to the agency and the first few modeling dates. No one will think you are less competent or not grown-up enough if you bring your mother or father with you.

Dan Deeley says it like this: "There are all kinds of people in this world and we know that, so we have to sit our young people down and tell them the facts. We tell them they could come up against problems but that they don't have to do anything unsavory to help their careers. We want them to understand these things, so we're pretty direct and frank. The first time Kevin came down to see us, his mother came with him. Later, I met his father. His mother went with him on his first three assignments. We encourage that."

A legitimate print agency will expect you to sign a contract that says you will work only for them. Since you are a minor, your parents will also have to sign. Once you have an agreement, the agency will begin to set up appointments for photographers to see you. Usually you will be expected to pay for your own transportation to interviews and go-sees. Once you begin earning money, the agency will get a commission on your work. For print photography, that is usually about twenty percent.

The agency will place you on the testing board. Your primary job at that level is to visit as many photographers as possible. If you get a favorable response from some of them, you will begin to get work.

Next comes the promotion board. You will still be

visiting photographers, perhaps better-known ones, and you will also be visiting potential clients.

The final step for a model is the high board. There you can expect to earn really good money and work several times a week. The top models that you read about who earn such high amounts of money are all on the high board.

Some girls never make it past the testing board. Others stop at the promotion board, working occasionally and hoping to make it to the high board. After a period of time, perhaps two or three years, their work might fall off and they might be dropped altogether. If they aren't getting all the work they want and the agency still believes they have the potential to become top-earning models, the agency might send them to Europe or Japan to see if that will give their careers a boost.

The agency's basic responsibility is to send you out for interviews for possible jobs and collect the money you earn. Beyond that, the agency will try to guide your career and give you basic training. Your responsibility is to be available for work at the agreed times and to perform your jobs to the best of your ability. Both you and the agency have a right to drop out of the agreement if it doesn't work out. Sometimes an agency will drop a girl after a few months if she doesn't get enough work. Sometimes a model will switch agencies if she feels another one can do a better job for her.

The agency is the first big step in a would-be model's career. How well she does depends on: how good the agency is; her own natural ability; her business sense; her persistence, ambition, timing, and luck.

Chapter 5

Should You Go to Modeling School?

Some young people who do not have an agency close to them or who feel they are not ready to approach an agency for professionals choose to go to modeling school.

Karen Wolff is a fifteen-year-old at Hudson High School in Hudson, New York. Several months ago, a woman from a local modeling school came to her home economics class to talk about modeling. Karen decided to sign up for modeling school.

"I'm five feet eleven inches tall and I would like to be a model when I'm older but I know there's a lot of competition," Karen says. "When I went to the school with my father for an interview, they were really nice. The woman at the school told us what school was like and that it would be a good experience — even to help with job interviews.

"In school, I learned about posture and makeup, and I got a lot more confidence in myself. I learned how to speak up and how to dress. Now I'm growing my fingernails. I feel different from before, and I dress up more.

"Another thing school did for me was make me more diet-conscious. I started out at 145 pounds and now I'm at 136. I hope to lose 10 more soon. There are other things I learned at school I couldn't do alone. I read a lot of books about modeling but I couldn't learn the runway walk alone. It is like learning a new dance. Hard work.

"So far, I have been in a fashion show the school arranged. I didn't get paid for that. I've also been in another show for Barbie dolls. I got $22.50 for that. On my own, I applied for a job at a bridal shop in my town. The woman said she would hire me later on. I'll be selling and modeling, I think. I don't know how much I'll make there.

"When I finish high school, I'll go to New York and try to be a model there. I may combine it with a career in retail merchandising. That's what I'm studying in school right now. Anyway, I'm glad I went to modeling school."

By Karen and her parents' accounting, they have invested close to $1,300 in her career so far. The tuition for modeling school was almost $900. They bought clothes, including high-heeled pumps. They had a tailored suit made to fit Karen and bought some other dresses. The transportation back and forth to school is costly.

There are still the photographs to buy for Karen's

portfolio, but her mother is taking pictures of every event that Karen participates in. Some of those will go into her first portfolio. Like her daughter, Mrs. Wolff is happy that Karen has enrolled in modeling school. She says, "I just hope she can get some good-paying jobs from it. But if not, she still has had the experience, which was good."

The money that the Wolffs spent is not unusual. Modeling school tuition can be very expensive and most of the graduates never earn enough money from modeling to pay it off. For that reason, modeling schools are sometimes called dishonest. If they make the claim that all their graduates will become professional models, that is certainly not true, but most schools are careful about what they promise. Since most of them are regulated by state agencies, they are careful not to say that they can get you modeling jobs after you graduate. Instead, they talk about the benefits that the school can offer and hint that their school is the fastest way to a modeling career. Many doubt that.

Claudia Black at Ford has this to say about these schools: "A modeling school is helpful if the girl has no poise and she knows absolutely nothing. If you've got a twelve-year-old and she's a tomboy and suddenly she wants to be a woman but doesn't know how to go about it, then a modeling school will help her. They'll teach her makeup, how to walk, and how to coordinate outfits. But that may not make her a good model."

One top model who asked not to be named had this to say: "Around my agency and in New York, telling them that you went to a modeling school is

46

sort of a joke. But I went and I know it helped me. My advice to girls who want to work as models and who need to gain confidence is to go, but don't tell the big agencies when you apply for a job."

This model's confession is in direct contrast to the opinions of most of the executives of the top agencies. Generally, they believe that *the agency* can instruct a girl if she has natural ability. As Louise Roberts of Prestige puts it, "We teach them everything they need to know. We give them seminars on street behavior, on makeup, and on how to act at interviews. We teach them how to dress and how to do their own hair. We teach them how to sell themselves and their best features."

Whether you go to a modeling school or not is a decision you must make carefully with your parents' advice and cooperation. Since most schools have high tuition, it usually means that your parents will have to help you pay for the lessons. Often, they will be involved in transporting you to and from the school as well.

There are modeling schools in most medium-sized towns and all of the larger ones. Some of the schools are part of a chain such as Barbizon, which has eighty-two schools in the United States. Other schools are owned and operated by individuals, usually a retired model. Occasionally modeling courses are given at local community centers, YWCAs, or Girls' Clubs.

Each school is different and has a different tuition fee. The courses taught in local community centers may be as inexpensive as twenty dollars for six weeks of lessons. In 1982, the basic price for a Barbizon modeling course of sixty hours was $895. While it is impossible to say for sure, there is no reason to believe that an expensive course will necessarily be more helpful than an inexpensive one. Before you choose a school, check out the teacher's background and experience. Find out what sort of modeling work she has done and where she did it. If the course is an expensive one, ask to sit in on a trial lesson. Perhaps you could ask to talk to graduates who have gone on to modeling work. Be careful. Be cautious and remember that the money you spend might be the money you need for the big trip into the city if an agency contacts you. Is school really the best way to further your career? Only you can decide for sure.

Above all, remember that graduating from a modeling school does not absolutely guarantee you modeling work. Even if the school has an agency connected with it, that may not be much help if you haven't got the right look or they haven't got the right jobs to offer. So if the school promises to register you with their agency, you should realize that it isn't quite the same thing as being taken on by a regular modeling agency.

Most modeling schools offer standard courses in grooming, cosmetics, runway walking, hair care, and speaking for television commercials. As an example of what you might expect, the Barbizon course is given over a period of twenty weeks and consists of sixty hours of instruction. That means that you would be attending school one night a week for three hours for twenty weeks. Each night, you would have a course in one aspect of modeling. That might be experimenting with different hairstyles one week and practicing walking on a runway the next. Usually, students would have the same teachers from week to week, though some lessons might be taught by teachers who are expert at one phase of modeling. The teachers should all have had some modeling experience, though they might not necessarily be persons who earned their living that way.

Steve L. Murray, administrator of the Barbizon School of Albany, New York, says, "Less than ten percent of our graduates go on to modeling careers, but a hundred percent benefit from our course." If you have the money to spend, modeling schools may be helpful, but they may not be the best way to start your career. You should also know that the fee you pay for schooling doesn't necessarily include photographs. At Barbizon, one 11" x 14" photo is included in the course cost. The school arranges a photography session for you and you may choose to purchase other photos. The average that students spent for extra photos was $300, according to Mr. Murray.

Again, it is important to understand that signing up with a modeling school is not the same as signing with an agency. No matter what the school officials say your chances for a modeling career are, they are making their money from your school fees, not from your modeling fees. Just as you should be wary of agencies who charge fees to register you, you should be careful of schools who charge fees to teach you. While they are probably legitimate, they may not be the best way to spend your money.

You may learn some important skills in modeling school but many of those skills can be learned on your own. Of course, you will want to check to see if your local community center or schools are offering inexpensive courses in modeling. Even if there are no such courses, there may be related classes that can help you. Does your local school have a television course? You can prepare yourself for television work by learning to operate a camera and speak in front of it. Both behind-the-camera work and performing will be good experience.

Watching people on television commercials and trying to imitate their manner at the mirror can be a good beginning. So can reading aloud to your younger brothers and sisters or volunteering to read to the blind. The important thing is to speak clearly and with animation. Even if a modeling school offers you three or six hours of practice, you would have to do more on your own.

Your posture can be improved by exercise or an inexpensive yoga course at the YWCA. Experimentation with cosmetics and hairstyling comes naturally to most teenagers. Diet and exercise can do more for your skin and general appearance than twenty years of modeling school. In other words, you can teach yourself a lot on your own.

If you feel that you need the extra push that a school will give you before you tackle the agencies, why not check out the possibility of private classes from an ex-model who lives close to you? Perhaps she can help you for a small fee.

If you are going to be a successful model, you will need a legitimate agency. The most direct route is to apply to the agencies nearest you. If there are not any agencies or if you need to prepare yourself for your modeling career before you tackle the agencies, you might consider a modeling school. Or you may want to save your money and get your training in other ways. Models need to be practical about money and clever about learning things on their own. It is never too early to begin to develop these characteristics.

Chapter 6

What About Small Towns?

Not all modeling agencies are in New York or Los Angeles, California, though a large percentage of the print and television modeling is done there. Certainly, those two cities are where the biggest money can be earned. *Time* magazine reported in the February 9, 1981, issue that 5,000 of the 15,000 models in New York City make $60,000 to $80,000 a year. They said that the top 120 models made up to $150,000 and about 60 top, top models earned $350,000 annually. However, these top earners are seldom teenagers. Most of them are high-fashion adults who have been modeling for several years. Just being in a big city does not guarantee earning big money.

Other large cities such as Chicago, Miami, and Dallas are also big centers for modeling. If you live within an hour and a half of one of these secondary markets, your first step is to send your photo and measurements to every agency you find listed in the Yellow Pages of that city. Many models work in cities of this size for their whole careers and do very well. As a teen, you might expect to find part-time work in these secondary markets.

Other cities such as Phoenix, Tucson, San Francisco, Denver, Atlanta, Boston, Detroit, Minneapolis, Kansas City, Las Vegas, Cleveland, Cincinnati, Philadelphia, Houston, and Montreal, Canada, have one or more busy modeling agencies. They do work with local television stations, local and national magazines, as well as fashion show and personal appearance work. Karen David, assistant director of the Dorien Leigh Modeling Agency in Cleveland, Ohio, had this to say about the kind of work they had to offer, in a *Seventeen* magazine article of June, 1979: "Only about twenty-five to thirty-five percent of our calls are for models to wear clothing in fashion shows or display a manufacturer's line to store buyers. The rest are for print work outside the fashion field, trade shows, and commercials."

While these secondary markets seldom have enough business to offer full-time work to many models, there may be enough work for teens who are still in school. Combining school activities and part-time modeling works well for many teens who live near these secondary markets. For example, Barbara Eagle, a sixteen-year-old from Cleveland, Ohio, got a part-time job posing in the snow for a group of holiday greeting cards. As she reported in *Seventeen* magazine, "We were driven from one scenic area to another, and we took walks, had snowball fights, and did anything else the photographer could think of."

Perhaps you live too far away from any large city to commute for part-time jobs. You may have to settle for part-time free-lancing and hope to move to a larger center after high school. Sometimes a model can achieve a different kind of compromise if her parents are willing to help her. You read that Sarah Duffey began her modeling career in Minneapolis and then spent two summers in New York City with her mother while she was still in high school. Her parents were able to support her plans for a modeling career with money and time. The fact that she had been getting work in Minneapolis made it seem practical to them.

Sometimes girls will have a relative or close friend of the family who lives in a larger city. It might be possible to send photos to agencies in that city and say that summer work is wanted. If the agency is interested, they may take a girl on for the summers and Christmas vacations with the understanding that she will move to the city after high school. Few agencies will urge a girl to move before then. As Claudia Black of Ford says, "The best way to begin is to do the local work. Get your tear sheets, get whatever magazines are done locally. Then send your pictures and say you're interested in coming for the summer. If they're interested, they'll let you know."

While you may hope to move to a larger city eventually, any modeling experience you can get in your community will be helpful. If there is a shopping center close to you, call and find out what agency the stores use to do their fashion shows. Contact that agency, no matter how small it is. Even if you are not paid for your first jobs, you will be gaining experience and poise. All experience can be valuable.

One of the department stores near you may have a teen board. Or perhaps they hire teens to model part-time while they are selling cosmetics. Maybe that job is for you. Don't forget that most modeling jobs are this sort of work, not the fabulous high-paying work you read about in magazines.

If you are near a college or school of photography, you might find work as a photographer's model. One successful teen model, Kajsa Ceder, started her modeling career by posing part-time for a local school of photography. She lived in Santa Barbara, California, which is too far away from Los Angeles for daily work. While she prepared for her full-time modeling career, she was also active on her high school drill team. Her three hours of work each day kept her in shape for her future modeling jobs.

As a senior in high school, Kajsa approached a top Los Angeles agency and began to take on important modeling assignments. In February, 1981, *Teen* magazine did a feature story on her and she gave this advice to beginning models: "Keep your head on straight and look at modeling in perspective. The photographers and everyone will tell you you're great and beautiful, but you have to remember you're in front of a camera. You can't go off thinking everyone feels the same way about you or you'll get a really big head. Hang on to your own personality and values, because that's what's important."

As soon as she graduated from high school, Kajsa planned to move to Los Angeles to expand her modeling career, but she had made a very good start on it in the smaller town of Santa Barbara. Her story is typical of small-town girls who model part-time and then move on to the bigger cities.

Suppose you live so far out in the country that you are more than two hours from any city at all? Your closest shopping mall is three hours away and there is no school of art or photography near you? Though few Americans live in such remote areas, there are rural communities like this.

If you are really that isolated, you may have to create your own opportunities and do the best you can as a free-lancer until you are out of high school. You can organize fashion shows for organizations in your town. Perhaps your local Women's Clubs or 4-H Clubs would be interested in your ideas.

Don't overlook the possibility of contests that you can enter. Sometimes magazines have cover girl contests, and you should certainly send your photograph into any of those. You might also enter any local beauty contests that would bring you publicity. Remember that Dan Deeley said his agency was always on the lookout for contest winners. Entering contests, whether they are the local Miss America tryouts or the Queen of the Witherspoon Rodeo, will give you poise and help you assess your chances at a modeling career. Win or lose, the experience can be valuable.

Nearly every community, no matter how remote, has a newspaper and that newspaper has some local advertising. While most ads that contain photographs are created in large cities, there may be some opportunities to pose for local advertisers. Contact the advertising manager of your local paper. He or she will be happy to talk to you and may have some ideas about how to further your career.

Above all, read everything you can about modeling, about advertising and fashion. You will have a head start on the girl who doesn't know what she wants to do until it happens. You can learn a lot by yourself and wait for your chance to put that learning into practice. Watch your local television news and read your local newspaper. Follow up anything that looks likely. Your hard work will pay off sooner or later.

If you have a specialty, you may be able to build a career around that. Ken Bailey was a teenager in Colorado when he started his modeling career. His big break came through skiing, and he's still doing a lot of television and print assignments that require athletic ability.

"I was still a teenager when a photographer saw me skiing and asked me if I'd ever modeled. That got me my first modeling job. I spent five days skiing in Vail, Colorado, while they photographed me. It was fun and the money was great. So naturally, I thought I would try to find more assignments."

A lover of the great outdoors, Ken has worked his way through college with the money he's made around the Denver, Colorado, area. Now he's in New York City working as a model and taking courses in filmmaking and communications, but he began his career as a small-town boy with a special talent.

Whatever special talents you have, develop them. Any athletic ability should be encouraged because models need to be strong and supple. If you have dramatic ability, do all the theater work you can. You will have your chance at a modeling career if you work hard to develop your potential.

Chapter 7

What About Television?

Making television commercials is one way models earn a lot of money. Though they may make less than a model's wages for the first day's work, the future prospects are great. If the commercial is a national and runs over a period of time, the model might make several thousand dollars through payment of residual fees. Each time the commercial is run, the principal actors earn extra money and that money is called *residuals*.

Because commercial work is so high paying, there is a lot of competition for it. Not only do models try out for commercials but so do actors and actresses. "It is really freaky to try out against the big stars," one model confessed. "It makes it a whole different ball game."

Working in television nearly always means living

in or close to New York or Los Angeles. There are a few local commercials made in secondary cities, but over ninety percent of the commercials you see on your television screen were booked in one of the two centers, New York or Los Angeles. Often a commercial is made on location, but the crew and models are flown in.

Television usually requires that models talk as well as look pretty. One of the first things that a model who wants to work on television has to do is get rid of any accent she might have. Since most television commercials are used nationwide, advertisers want people who sound as though they might come from any part of the country.

The people who are used on television are often more "real" looking than print models. While most commercials use attractive people, they usually have a quality that is described as *The Girl Next Door*. However, cosmetic commercials and other expensive products often use the most glamorous models they can find.

Almost from the beginning of her modeling career, Lynea Forseth began to get commercial work. For Lynea, those jobs mean money in the bank for her college education. She wants to do as much work in television as she can, not only because of the money, but because she finds it challenging.

"I started going out for commercials as soon as I could. My first one was a Pepsi commercial where all I had to do was look young and happy. That was a lot of fun. The commercials pay well and I've always been interested in acting.

"For the auditions, I wear very natural makeup, T-shirts, and jeans. They want to see you as the all-

American kid, so it's best not to be fancy. Generally, the people who come to auditions don't dress up. It isn't a rule, but it is sort of the custom.

"On commercial auditions, they put you on film and they give you cue cards. You sometimes have a few minutes to look the script over and sometimes you don't. You just interpret it as best you can. They decide on your looks, on how you fit the product, and how you act.

"One commercial I did was for Impulse toothpaste, and for that one, I was supposed to be younger — about thirteen. But for most of them, I'm supposed to be my age — sixteen. I guess I have the kind of face that looks healthy and young, and I hope I'll keep that look for several years so I can do this kind of work through college.

"I just did a commercial that required some real acting. In it, I was supposed to be one of those Valley Girls. I had a pack of gum in my mouth and made my voice slide up and down. It was kind of funny. For that one, I had to do some research. I read up on Valley Girls and listened to the Moon Unit Zappa record. I'd never heard it before. Anyway, it was great fun."

Like Lynea, most models try to combine television and print careers if they are in locations that make it possible. Though Lynea plans a career in medicine, many other models hope to move from modeling into acting or some related business. You have heard that Tracey Ross and Sarah Duffey both have careers in acting as their long-term goals. Howard Balaban is already acting and plans to eventually get into filmmaking. So does Ken Bailey. While all these young models may not fulfill their ambitions, their hopes illustrate how closely connected the acting and modeling businesses really are.

Like some of the other modeling agencies, Wilhelmina has a separate department that represents its models for commercials and acting jobs. This talent department manages the model's career. When a model is first signed up, the talent department brings her in for an audition that is exactly like a casting call. During the audition, the talent specialists observe the weak and strong points of the new model. Then they suggest the classes that the model should take to develop her potential for a television career.

Getting television jobs is more complicated than obtaining print assignments. Though print modeling agencies often get calls from casting companies and send their girls out on auditions, not all of them have separate television talent departments. Many print agencies expect that their models will also be registered with several different television agencies and casting companies.

The television commercial companies do not expect a model to sign an exclusive contract with them since the business is very different from the print modeling business. Television agencies may get calls from casting companies or from advertising agencies that they work with. Not all television agencies get all calls so it is important for a model to register with as many as possible. Claudia Black of Ford describes this aspect of the business this way: "There are literally thousands of people out there on the casting end of television so it makes sense to free-lance."

Another complication in getting television work is that often the descriptions of what advertisers want are very vague. The advertising agency may send out a call for a young blonde and actually hire an older redhead. A girl who is registered with several different agencies has a better chance to be sent out on the audition by one of them.

Television agencies charge fees of ten percent. Once a model has done two commercials, she will have to join one of the actors' unions — either AFTRA (American Federation of Television and Radio Actors) or SAG (Screen Actors Guild).

Many models who work in television select managers to help them with their careers. The manager charges another twenty percent, which means that the model is paying thirty percent of her earnings to her agent and manager, but most girls who are really active in television believe it is worth it.

A manager will decide whether or not the model should go to an audition. He or she will also guide a teen's career so that the high earning years really pay off. As Claudia Black points out, "If a kid is hot in TV — and there are kids who can make two hundred thousand a year — it's worth the thirty percent."

Selecting a manager and registering with television agencies usually comes after you have some experience in other types of modeling. Managers and television talent agencies can be found in the Yellow Pages or by asking your representative at your modeling agency.

Television work often goes to the girl with the most experience. For that reason, many beginners take television commercial classes or acting classes. Since the fields of acting and commercials are so close, some girls select acting classes if that is their eventual goal. Others who are only interested in modeling choose to go to the commercial classes.

Claudia Black advises, "Anyone who's interested in this business should get any experience she can right away. Some kids are naturals, but most need experience. Remember, you'll be up against kids who are actors, too."

One of the reasons that television work is so attractive to teenagers is that the size requirements are not as strict. Often a girl's print career is over at seventeen if she hasn't reached five feet seven inches in height. Once she looks too old for the teen department, she'll be dropped because high fashion work demands that extra height. In television, height is not that important.

"We had a teen model who didn't grow," says Claudia Black. "She was a perfect example of a beautiful girl who became sixteen and was still only five feet three. She knew she wouldn't be doing anything in print, but she had so many talents. She's a violinist, a ballet dancer, and has starred in plays. So she got more involved in acting and now she's starring in a soap opera. Her name is Cindy Gibb."

More than one teenage model has gone from television commercials to acting in soap operas. Two years after Cusi Cram was the subject of a *Seventeen* magazine story about her first modeling job, she was acting in a soap opera on a regular basis. Like many teen models, her interest in acting had started early. At thirteen, when she started modeling, she already was taking acting lessons and had some local stage and film experience.

Brooke Shields is the most famous teen who has combined print modeling and acting. She started modeling when she was one year old and made her first movie at age nine. She starred in a movie at age eleven and had eight films to her credit by the time she was sixteen. But her modeling career is just as important as her acting career, and *Time* magazine reported in the February 9, 1981, issue that her modeling fees were as high as $10,000 a day. They also said she was about to sign a $1 million contract with Calvin Klein to continue advertising his jeans.

Though few models or actresses ever make that kind of money or achieve the kind of fame that Brooke Shields has, her career demonstrates the way television modeling and acting can be combined.

Another reason some models find television so attractive is that the characters that are used on television are often not as gorgeous as in print work. Even if her features are not perfect, if she is attractive and can deliver her lines well, a model may have a chance at television work. "In TV," says Claudia Black, "they are looking for character. Good Old Boy, Down-home Girl, Cheerleader Cute — that type of thing. If you can put character in it and deliver the words in the script, you have a chance."

Preparation for television work is complicated if you don't live in a big city or can't afford to take acting and commercial classes. School plays, amateur theatrics, and public speaking all help develop the speaking habits and poise necessary for television work. Any practice you get in front of a television screen will be very helpful. Many schools now have television equipment and most towns have small cable companies that do local shows. Investigate all the possibilities if you have television modeling as your goal in the future.

Chapter 8

Is Modeling Good for You?

As you can see, modeling is hard work that may pay off financially if you are especially attractive, talented, or lucky. Since the competition is so great, there are many young people who will try for modeling careers and never make it. They may be willing to work hard and be very good looking but fail anyway.

"Modeling, like any business, is luck," says Claudia Black. "Are they interested in your look this year? There are trends and maybe you won't be right today but ten years ago, your look would have been perfect. Nobody knows until she tries, but be prepared for rejection and remember that you're still a good person."

Other girls will have some success as models and find that the business really isn't for them. Sometimes they find the work boring. One schoolteacher who had done some modeling when she was younger had this to say about the work: "It was just plain boring. I would go into a sort of daze when I modeled for art classes. Sometimes I had to hold poses for thirty minutes and my muscles would ache for hours. Later, I was in some television commercials and they did the same thing over and over. Once I ran across a porch and picked up a little kid forty times before they got the shot they wanted. Modeling would never satisfy me, no matter how much they paid me."

Successful models also find the work boring or physically difficult at times, but they adjust. Well-known high fashion model Carol Alt was quoted in a *New York* magazine article about supermodels as saying, "I'm investing. If I've got to stand in the cold in a bathing suit, or in the heat in furs, I want something to show for it." Like most models who make it big, she is interested in the financial rewards that modeling brings her, so she is willing to put up with the difficult physical demands of the job.

There are models who work for a while and then drop out of the field because they find the rejection too painful. Robin Jewell, model editor at *Seventeen* magazine, is an ex-model herself. She has this to say about rejection: "You go on a call and they want blondes. You're a blonde but you open the door and there are fifty other blondes. Some are prettier than you and some of them aren't. It's a very, very competitive business. I think it hurts the girls who take it too seriously. If you really get caught up in it, then it can make you insecure. But if you can have fun with it, then it's good for you."

Handling rejection — whether it results from trying out for a part in the school play, asking a favorite boy to the dance, or missing out on the part in the Pepsi commercial — can be very painful. Nevertheless, rejection is a part of life and no one can totally avoid it. Those people who try to escape rejection by never attempting anything are probably the unhappiest people in the world. However, in modeling there is more rejection than in other activities. If you are very sensitive and have a hard time with rejection, modeling may not be for you.

Lynea Forseth has learned to live with rejection as she goes on her rounds each day looking for modeling jobs. She says, "Of course you have to be able to handle rejection if you're going to be happy. If I compared myself to Brooke Shields all the time, I could be miserable. But I'm my own person and she's her own person. I'm doing what I do and she's doing what she does. I feel that's very important to realize. Otherwise, you would be unhappy all the time."

Because the competition is so tough and so many girls are disappointed, your friends may try to discourage you from trying to become a model. Many girls find it is easier not to talk about their modeling activities too much in school. "It's hard enough to believe in yourself," one young beginner said. "I sure don't want to hear a lot of warnings and discouraging advice from other people."

Even after they've started their careers, some girls avoid talking about it too much in school. "I don't want them to think I'm stuck-up," one girl admitted. Another said, "It doesn't really do any good to talk about my work at school. Most kids have such unrealistic ideas about modeling. They think I get to keep all the clothes, for instance. Silly stuff like that."

If you want to become a model so that other people will look up to you, or to prove that you are prettier than the other girls in your school, then modeling will not be good for you. The most common criticism of models is that they are stuck-up or self-centered. While this is not true of most of the hard-working professionals, it may be true of some beginners.

Another criticism of models is that they are dumb and never think about anything but how they look. As you can see from the interviews with models in this book, that is not so. Models are just like any other group of people except they are exceptionally attractive in appearance. Some are smart and some are not so smart, but most of them who last long in the business have enough intelligence to manage their careers successfully.

Teenage models often use their modeling money to pay for college courses so that they can go into other careers after their modeling days are over. Since modeling careers are so short, most young women understand that they will have to find other work. Some go into the theater and others go into related fields such as photography, makeup styling, advertising, or television production.

"The dumb ones don't survive," one modeling executive said. "But if a girl is smart, she can use the contacts she makes and the money she saves to build a good life."

Some people think it is silly to waste your time trying to be a model when your career will obviously be so short. While it is true that most models work only three to five years, and a very good career usually lasts about ten years, that trend does seem to be changing. Especially with television commercial success, you may be able to prolong your career indefinitely. "One of our girls started at nineteen doing high fashion print," says Louise Roberts of Prestige. "She's thirty-five now and doing TV commercials where she plays the housewife and mother. She's got talent and she's got a half a million in securities and cash."

In the last few years, supermodels like Cheryl Teigs, Lauren Hutton, and Christina Farrare have all been earning large fees at age thirty and older. One very elegant model named Carmen is now fifty and still modeling high fashion clothing. She is the exception. While some top names are older, the high-fashion modeling business is still a short career for most girls.

The modeling agency will want to know that your parents are going to be backing your career. Claudia Black puts it this way: "The most important thing with a teenager or child is the parent behind her. A parent can make or break a kid in this business. Many a kid has been turned down because there's no interest on the parent's part. You just can't expect a fourteen-year-old to arrange her schedule and get herself to jobs without help."

If your parents are doubtful about your ability to be a model, you may be able to convince them after some small successes. Perhaps your performance at a local fashion show or a letter from an agency in response to your photo will change their minds.

Sometimes parents are very definitely against the idea of their child modeling. If this is the case, listen carefully to their objections. Perhaps they are afraid of the life that they think models lead. You may be able to share some of the information you've read in this book with them. Perhaps they are discouraging you because they don't want you to be hurt. If that is the case, you can talk to them about how you feel about rejection. With time, you and your parents may come to the decision that you can start looking for local modeling work. Or you may agree that it is a good idea to send your photo to a few modeling agencies and let them decide if you have the potential.

The decision to try for a teenage modeling career is one that you and your parents will have to make together. You may choose to delay your attempts until you are out of school, either because you are too far away from the modeling centers or because you think it will interfere with school. In some cases, that may be the sensible decision, since modeling does mean missing days at school for important jobs.

Any young woman who decides she wants to try for a career as a model must understand that it is hard work and she has to be very serious about it. "Teens need to be aware that it means discipline and giving up a lot," warns Claudia Black. "There's no time for movies and cheerleading and no chocolate sundaes after school. For most kids, I'd say don't try for it. There are so many problems in the teen years that they don't need the extra grief. There's tests and boys and learning who you are. So unless it really means a lot to you, let it go."

On the other hand, most teenage models who are successful feel that their work has helped them in many ways. "I'm much more poised," one said. Another claims that modeling has actually helped her focus better on her schoolwork. "I just know that time is very important and now I use it better."

Whether modeling is good for you is something you will have to decide for yourself. The checklist below will help you make that decision, because it covers some of the basic requirements for successful modeling. As photographer Owen Brown says, "Modeling can be very good for a girl or very destructive. It depends on how the girl relates to it. I've seen some girls thrive on it. Others get so wrapped up in themselves that they are ruined. Attitude is the whole thing."

Ask yourself . . .

How do I react when I get turned down for things?

Am I more sensitive than other people?

Do I hate to be criticized?

Can I take orders easily?

Do I get bored easily?

Can I concentrate for long periods of time?

Do I worry how I look all the time?

Do I want to be prettier than everyone else?

Do I need others to admire me all the time?

Do I have good grades in school?

How good are my study habits?

Can I stick to something when I start it?

What do friends think about my modeling?

How important are their opinions to me?

What do my parents think about modeling?

Can I listen to their opinions carefully?

Do I have real determination to be a model?

How much do I want it?

What is my attitude toward other people?

Would modeling be good for me?

Chapter 9

Could You Be a Model?

Many young girls often dream of becoming models. Those who are considered especially pretty by their friends and families are sometimes urged to pursue a modeling career. While having a pretty face is an asset in modeling, it is not the most important consideration. And having a face that is considered beautiful is not a guarantee that a girl will be successful as a model.

When you are considering a modeling career, you must try and be realistic about your chances. Remembering that the competition is keen, you can take a good, strong look at yourself and your potential before you begin. While you are trying to decide whether or not you could be a model, it is important to keep in mind that there are some things that you can change and others that you cannot.

A pretty face may or may not be photogenic. Some girls who do not seem to be exceptionally pretty make the best fashion models of all. "They have that certain quality I call the x factor," says Louise Roberts of Prestige.

Time magazine described the appearance of top fashion model Clotilde as she arrived for work in this way: " . . . a plain-faced, skinny young woman." They went on to quote Clotilde as saying about herself, "I'm an optical illusion." While being pretty is no guarantee of modeling success, having a face that photographs well is important for fashion print work.

Generally, wide-set eyes, full lips, and high cheekbones are important in photographic work. Many photographers prefer to work with girls who have light-colored eyes as well. Whether or not your face is suitable for print work may not be easy for you to judge. This checklist may help, but the definite answer will have to come from the modeling agencies you contact.

Do I . . .
Look good in most photographs?
Have high cheekbones?
Have a good, strong nose?
Have regular features?
Have wide-set eyes?
Have a full mouth?
Have something special about my face?

You do not have to answer yes to all those questions in order to have a chance at a print modeling career, but they may help you decide.

Of course, there are many things you can change

about your face through good health habits and makeup, but you cannot change your basic bone structure or your features. While makeup and skin care will help you make the best of what you have, it probably will not make you photogenic if you are not. That is why it is so important to let the experts decide, even if you think your face is not as pretty as those you see in magazines.

Remember that print work is only one aspect of modeling. Even if it is clear that you are not photogenic enough for fashion work in magazines, you can have a great career in runway or personal appearance modeling. If you have a face that does not photograph as beautiful or even pretty, you may still have a career in "character" modeling, especially if you have talent that will come across on television.

Judging your face is only one part of making the judgment about whether or not you could be a model. There are other very important considerations. Your height and body type can be just as important as your face.

To be a high fashion model, you will have to be at least five feet seven inches tall. Most models are five feet nine and some are as tall as five feet eleven. Since you have no control over how tall you grow, your modeling career is subject to the dictates of nature. Though a few models, like Sarah Duffey, pursue a modeling career even though they are only five feet six, it is very difficult. The camera makes people look shorter and heavier than they really are. For that reason, photographers choose to work with long, slim body types in fashion photography.

You may still be growing and not know how tall you will be as an adult. Even if you are short, if you are a young-looking twelve- to fourteen-year-old, you may be able to model preteen or junior clothes. Agencies are interested in very young girls for these jobs because the careers are so short. Most girls look too old at sixteen for these fashions. Perhaps by the time you are too adult looking, you will have grown into the height required.

Some teens model junior fashions with only five feet six or seven inches of height. Mary Beth Hoey is getting lots of work as a teen model, but she fears her career will be short unless she grows another inch or two. By the time she is eighteen or nineteen, she will probably look too old for teen clothes. Whether she moves into the world of high fashion is out of her control, since there is nothing she can do to grow taller.

Junior models look young and are usually five feet six or seven inches tall. They wear size five or size seven clothes. Like all fashion models, they must have slim, well-proportioned bodies. Large breasts or hips are out.

Regular models who are five feet seven to five feet eleven inches tall must also be very slim. Their bodies must appear softly rounded and healthy. A few years ago, many models looked very, very thin, but that has gone out of style. This look, called "the asparagus look" by John Casablancas, head of Elite Model Management, has been replaced by vigorous good health. Today's models must look alive, healthy, and full of vitality.

Do you have a fashion model's figure? Are you tall and slim in basic body type? To give you some comparison, page 76 lists some measurements published by *Seventeen* magazine for top teen models.

Jayne Modean

Height	5′ 9″
Weight	114-117 lbs
Bust	34
Waist	24
Hips	34
Size	7-8-9

Cassandra

Height	5′ 7 1/2″
Weight	106-110 lbs
Bust	34
Waist	24
Hips	34
Size	7-8-9

Michele Stevens

Height	5′ 10″
Weight	115-118 lbs
Bust	34
Waist	24
Hips	34
Size	9-10

Your Statistics

Height	_____
Weight	_____
Bust	_____
Waist	_____
Hips	_____
Size	_____

As you compare your measurements, height, and weight to these young models' statistics, remember that you can change some things about yourself. In time, exercise and diet will add or subtract inches. However, if you are a young woman who has large bones and wide shoulders and hips, your basic body type may be wrong for fashion modeling. Most models are naturally slim and have small frames for their height. Though anyone can diet down to a smaller size, not everyone can achieve the model look. Too much dieting may leave you looking skinny and undernourished instead of slim and willowy. Your body type may naturally be shorter and wider than a fashion model's.

You will notice that the models' measurements are all perfectly proportioned. Their busts and hips are the same measurement. Their waists are ten inches smaller. This is considered the ideal proportion for fashion work. However, not all models are as perfectly proportioned as these girls are. Some are an inch or two larger in the bust or hips. Others have hips and busts that are nine or eleven inches larger than their waists. The important thing is to have a figure that is perfect enough so that the model can step right into clothing without any alterations being necessary.

You may want to take your own measurements and compare them with the ones you read about.

Remember that you can change some of your measurements through diet and exercise. The next chapter will give you tips and ideas on how to go about developing a model's figure. However, if your measurements seem to be very different from the proportions of the teen models, you may want to look realistically at your chances for a fashion career.

Even if your statistics are far from perfect, there

may be a place for you in the modeling business. If you live close to a large city, there may be work for you in television modeling where they use "real people." As long as you are an attractive person, you have a chance in that particular kind of work. You can be cute, fresh looking, happy-go-lucky looking, or even have a funny face and still make it on television if you have talent.

There may even be work for you in the print business if you can find an agency that specializes in supplying models for advertisers outside of the fashion field. Though most print work demands a particularly slim and gorgeous look, there are other kinds of models used in advertisements.

Browse through any of the general magazines you have in your home, particularly the ones with recipes for food. You will see photographs of older women tasting spaghetti while their hungry-and-cute-but-not-so-pretty kids watch eagerly. You will see happy-looking teens who are not beautiful sitting around the Thanksgiving table while Grandma brings in the turkey. These teens are all character models, and there is work for them. Some agencies specialize in character models. If your face has appeal but is not classically beautiful, you might think of character modeling.

Even if you are not beautiful, do not have a perfectly slim figure, and are not close to a television center or modeling agency that uses character faces, you may find work. If you move well, have an interesting face with strong features, and can hold poses for a long time, you might be an artist's model. Check with your local art schools and colleges to see if you qualify.

There are other modeling possibilities you might think about. If you have exceptionally pretty feet and legs, you might have a career as a model who specializes in shoe and hosiery advertisements. Every fashion agency has a few models who do nothing but foot or leg modeling. You will need long, slim legs, slender ankles, and a small shoe size. Most advertisers use size six shoes in their photographs.

Just as there are models with beautiful feet and legs, there are others who specialize in showing off their beautiful hands. Long, slender, perfectly formed hands with healthy, long nails might bring you a career modeling rings, wristwatches, or selling soap for dishwashing. Your glove size should be about a seven.

There may even be modeling work for the girl who is quite heavy. In recent years, the fashion industry has paid a lot of attention to fashions for larger women. Some stores, such as Forgotten Woman, specialize in selling clothes in size fourteen and larger. There are manufacturers of dresses that start at size sixteen. Some of these fashions are advertised in magazines and newspapers. The models who wear them are perfectly proportioned, pretty girls who wear a size sixteen or eighteen dress. There is even an agency in New York City that has only large-sized models. Look through the fashion magazines and see if you can spot some of the advertisements using these larger models.

Could you be a model? Look at yourself realistically and ask yourself whether you have the qualifications for one or more kinds of modeling. Ask yourself what you would like to change and what you cannot change. Realize that your chances are limited by accidents of growth, such as height and body type. Understand that just being pretty may not be enough. Then get ready to work on the qualities you have that might make you a career in the world of modeling. The last two chapters will show you how.

Chapter 10

Diet and Exercise Tips

Good health is the most important ingredient in a model's beauty package, all the experts agree. Shining hair, sparkling eyes, clear skin, and a slim body all depend on the proper combination of diet and exercise. Above all, it is important to remember that just being thin isn't enough. Slimness must be based on a sensible diet of the basic foods in the proper combination, not on crash dieting.

"Nothing is more dangerous to a teen's look than a starvation diet," one modeling agent stated flatly. "Dropping twenty pounds in thirty days can hurt your health and ruin your looks for months. The loss of nutrients will show up all over a girl's body. In her hair, skin, and muscle tone. Teens need decent food in the proper amounts to be pretty." Her sentiments were echoed by the other modeling executives and models.

A sound diet is made up of three satisfactory meals a day that combine the proper amounts of the basic four food types. To achieve slimness or to keep slim, a teen model might choose to eat larger amounts of vegetables and fruit but would also include some dairy products and some protein foods such as eggs, meat, or poultry in her diet.

Generally, successful models are careful not to eat foods that add calories and give little or no vitamins or minerals. "Junk foods are out," Claudia Black at Ford declares. "Any girl who is seriously interested in modeling knows that it means giving up chocolate-chip cookies or greasy French fries. Discipline is the key to good eating habits."

Most models don't think of themselves as being on a diet or giving up anything. They talk about getting the maximum amount of energy and good health out of their food choices. Supermodel Christie Brinkley has a brother who is a nutritionist and she has learned to follow his suggestions.

Another supermodel, Christina Ferrare, had to lose sixteen pounds after her baby was born. Because she was a smart dieter who didn't want to hurt her health, she took nine months to lose the weight. She was quoted in *Bazaar* magazine as saying, "I did it sensibly — otherwise, you get flabby and the pounds just come back."

Sound eating habits are something successful models aim for because they know that the nutrients in foods are responsible for their basic good looks. When models want to lose weight, they often do it by choosing smaller portions of healthful foods. Christie

Brinkley has this to say on the subject of dieting: "The sooner you realize there is no secret except cutting down, the sooner you're going to lose weight."

Tracey Ross is typical of the successful model who understands how to keep her diet healthy in all kinds of circumstances. "I know something about nutrition," she says. "And I like to do things as right as possible. I want to give my body everything that's good for it so I always carry something for a snack in my tote bag. An apple, usually. I have a yogurt on the train if I don't have time to eat lunch or if I'm in a hurry. The temptation to eat anything at all is too great when you're too hungry. So I find the key is not to let myself get that hungry."

While some models are able to eat larger amounts of food and not get fat, most of them are conscious of their weight all of the time. Lynea Forseth has this to say about her weight and attitude toward food: "I know with these cheeks of mine that I could be fat. So I have to be careful all of the time. I'm five feet six and weigh one hundred and seventeen pounds, and that's about right for my look. I wear a size three or five and that's good for teen modeling. But I really take care of myself. I exercise and get the right amount of sleep. I eat a well-balanced diet. I'd like to be a model for some time and I know this is the way to do it."

Your ideal weight depends on your body type, your look, and how solid your muscles are. At five feet six, Lynea Forseth weighs almost the same as Tracey Ross does at five feet eight. Yet both girls are perfect for their body type.

Some young women get overanxious about being slim when they begin their modeling careers. If you are interested in a modeling career and are on the light side of normal weight for your height, chances are that you are slim enough.

"I used to worry too much about my weight when I came into this business," Tracey Ross says. "I wasn't seeing myself realistically, so I dieted down to one hundred and fourteen pounds. I was almost too thin. I weigh a hundred and nineteen now and that's just right for my height and body structure. I would warn girls who want to model not to go overboard. Good looks are healthy looks."

Here are some tips for girls who would like to lose a few pounds and keep their good looks while they are doing it.

1. **Eat three complete meals a day.**
2. **Try not to snack. If you do, make it fruit.**
3. **Sweets and desserts are off limits.**
4. **Bread and cereal in small amounts are fine. Use whole wheat and whole grain products for greater nutrition.**
5. **Avoid sauces and gravies made with butter, oil, or cream.**
6. **Eat slowly and chew well. This makes smaller amounts last longer.**
7. **Drink lots of water — at least eight glasses a day.**
8. **Weigh yourself at the same time once a week.**
9. **Eat plenty of fruits and vegetables.**
10. **Don't use food to make yourself feel better when you are tired or upset. Exercise or do something soothing like taking a hot bath.**

If you have more than twenty pounds to lose, you will need professional advice about your diet. Check with your doctor, and then you may decide to join a group like Weight Watchers or the Diet Clinic. It helps to have a group to support you when you have a lot to lose.

Along with a healthy diet, getting enough sleep is essential for good looks. Though a model's life may sound glamorous, most girls go home to bed very early on the nights when they know they will be working in the morning. Even in very young girls, lack of sleep can make eyes look dull and puffy.

While it is true that people need different amounts of sleep — usually between seven and nine hours — it is also true that teens need more sleep than older people. Any teen who wants a modeling career should build a solid nine hours of sleep time into her schedule. That means time in bed with her eyes closed, not reading or listening to the radio. If you find you cannot sleep that long, the quiet resting will be almost as good for you. "Get your beauty sleep" is an old expression based on a solid truth.

Dan Deeley of Wilhelmina has a different piece of advice for young models: "In this business it's real important to take care of yourself. That means clean living habits. No drugs. No alcohol. You read about models who do a lot of partying, but the best ones are too smart. They want to keep their bodies and minds together so they live without drugs or alcohol."

Many of the male models who work with Deeley are ex-athletes from high school or college. He says that all his models are very involved with some sort of sports activity, whether it is running, weight lifting, swimming, or calisthenics. In Deeley's opinion, the very best way for a young man or woman to prepare for a modeling career is to be athletic.

"In the past ten years," he says, "the model look has become very healthy and very American. The women as well as the men have become more and more athletic. We've had world-class runners in the men's and women's departments. Everyone plays squash or jogs or something. They're dedicated athletes, putting in a couple of hours a day. Their look is healthy and wholesome. I think that's because Americans have become so health-conscious, and I think it's good."

Exercise is a part of nearly every model's life. Mary Beth Hoey works very hard at her routines for her marching band. Jane Modean swims, hikes, and plays tennis. Michele Stevens works out in a New York City health club now, but when she lived in Oklahoma, she skied, hiked, played tennis, and scuba dived. You've already read how skiing brought Ken Bailey into the modeling business.

Exercise can help a model hold the long poses she needs to hold for art classes. It can help her develop the grace she needs for runway walking. It can give her the energy and stamina she needs for the long photographic sessions. When she is on television, her supple and easy movements will help her sell the product she is advertising.

Robin Jewell at *Seventeen* magazine has this to say about exercise: "I think it is the very best preparation for a modeling career. Dance, athletics, anything that deals with movement is very, very good. If a person doesn't know how to move, she'll be stiff before the camera. An athletic model can jump up in the air in front of the camera if she has to. She can have fun with the poses. If she's athletic, she'll be natural and relaxed. I can't recommend it enough."

There are a lot of different kinds of exercise that a young woman can choose. Probably any sort of exercise is good for you if you do it for a consistent period of time. You might consider choosing more than one kind of exercise and alternating them for a well-rounded program. For instance, bicycling is particularly good for your legs, and you might want to add some swimming to keep your arms firm and supple.

Exercises like swimming, bicycling, and jogging will give you a fast workout in a short amount of time. You may find that you enjoy taking long walks or going to a yoga class more than doing active exercises. Probably a good exercise program will combine some heavy exercise like bicycling and running with some movement work like yoga or dance. One class in aerobic dance may give you both the workout you need and the bending and stretching for grace.

There are so many combinations of exercise plans that it is impossible to suggest them all. The important thing to remember is that the more exercise and movement work you get, the better off you are. Don't kid yourself into thinking that a thirty-minute exercise session once a week will give you what you need for a model's figure and health. Most models find an hour a day for some sort of exercise. So should you.

Experiment with different types of exercise until you find one or two activities that you really enjoy. Schedule those into your week. You need the action to get your circulation stimulated. That will give you clear skin and bright eyes. You need the slower, movement exercise to give you the grace you need for your modeling work.

Some models combine dance with jogging. Others use bicycling and swimming for the action and take yoga classes. Very busy models who have a hard time fitting exercise into their workdays may get up at six in the morning and jog before they go to work. That night, they may exercise for thirty minutes while they listen to a tape of relaxing music.

The important thing is to make exercise a permanent part of your life. Like model Kim Alexis, you may have to be flexible. In a *Mademoiselle* article, "Tips from Top Models," she said, "I try to make time for swimming after work every day. If not, I settle for running up the steps to my apartment." If something happens and you can't fit in your favorite form of exercise, do something else.

Many books on modeling give spot reducing exercises to help girls bring their measurements into perfect balance. While these exercises may work eventually, it is not enough to pick one exercise for reducing your hips and call that an exercise program. Exercise should do more than attack a spot of fat on a hip or thigh. It should tone your whole body and give you graceful good health.

Spot exercising can sometimes work if it is kept up over a long period of time, but do not expect instant results. If you don't diet, the time it will take you to lose an inch or two off your hips might be as much as a year. If you do diet, you will probably lose the weight all over. Remember that exercising in ways such as fast walking, running, bicycling, and swimming will also take inches off your hips and thighs, perhaps faster.

Beware of expensive health clubs that promise to help you lose inches without working very hard. Their machines may not do anything for you at all. Usually, those health clubs also suggest that you participate in their exercise classes. (That is where you may lose the inches.) However, you can get the same sort of exercise classes much less expensively at your local YWCA or community center. If you want to use spot exercising to work on a particular trouble spot, you can check a book out of the library and do the exercises at home.

If you are serious about a modeling career, you will have to be serious about following a sensible diet and exercise plan. Top teen models like Cuzi Cram stay at the top because of their rigorous discipline. Cuzi takes jazz dance classes to stay in shape, and her favorite snacks are fruit, cottage cheese, and herbal teas.

Other models use fresh fruit and honey for a high-energy snack. If weight is a problem, the honey will be replaced by yogurt. Learning to rely on healthy food and exercise for beauty and energy cannot begin too soon. Compare your own diet and exercise habits to those of the models you've read about.

MY DIET
Do I eat three meals a day?
Do I avoid junk foods like potato chips and greasy hamburgers?
Do I think about nutrition when I select foods?

Do I eat plenty of vegetables?
Do I eat plenty of fresh fruit?
Do I drink eight glasses of water or more each day?
Do I avoid sugary desserts?
Are my food portions sensible?
If I want to lose weight, do I take it slowly and carefully?
Do I follow my good diet rules all the time?

MY EXERCISE
Do I enjoy exercise?
What is my favorite kind of exercise?
What do I do well?
What can I do each day?
Am I taking a dance class?
Is there a dance class available near me?
How about yoga?
How can I add more active exercise to my life?
How can I add some slow movement work to my life?
Do I have a plan that includes at least an hour of exercise a day?

As you ask yourself these questions, remember that you can gradually change your health habits to match those of a professional model. Whether you choose to follow a modeling career or decide to follow different kind of work, your health habits will be the foundation of your beauty as well as helping to prevent illness and making you a happier person. Both diet and exercise are keys to successful living.

Chapter 11

Beauty Tips from Models

When you think of a model's appearance, what do you see in your mind's eye? A slim figure, graceful movements, clear skin, sparkling eyes, and lovely hair. All of these beauty basics can come from a healthy diet and exercise plan. You can have every one of those assets by taking care to follow the suggestions you read about in the last chapter.

Not only does the food you eat and the exercise you get produce results in your body movement and shape, but it affects your skin, hair, and eyes. A good diet can even help your nails grow longer and stronger. If you follow the diet and exercise plan you've prepared for even six months, you will discover that your appearance has improved tremendously. You may not have perfectly regular features, or even a perfectly proportioned body, but you will be beautiful in your own way. That is a guarantee, based on the knowledge of all the beauty experts and health practitioners combined.

No girl who ignores the basic health rules will look as good as she could with that discipline. Once you understand that diet and exercise are the keystones of good looks, you understand the most important rule. Add sparkling cleanliness to your list of good health habits and you know most of what it takes to be a real beauty.

Zoltan Rendessy, who is head of the modeling agency Zoli, described the successful model look this way for *Time* magazine: "Clean and healthy," he said. "I tell my girls to look antiseptic — clean, clean, clean."

Other executives of modeling agencies agree with Zoltan's analysis of the perfect look for the eighties. Louise Roberts of Prestige has this to say about what her agency looks for in a new model: "We want her to look young, clean, and healthy. We look for someone who is copper-penny fresh."

Since the eighties' look is so fresh and healthy, a girl who wants to be a model should be very careful about the kind of makeup she uses. While most models do use makeup on the street, they learn to apply it with a very light hand. Especially girls who want to work as teen models must learn to keep their makeup young and attractive.

Mary Beth Hoey has this advice for girls who want to follow in her footsteps as a teen model: "If you're going into the city for a job, you want to look casual. They're interested in your face, not your clothes or your makeup. The less makeup you wear, the better. It should really blend in and not look phoney. I wear very light makeup because I know they want me to look young and innocent."

The advice that Mary Beth gives is seconded by Robin Jewell at *Seventeen* magazine. "Basically, try not to go to extremes. Keep an eye on what's going on in fashion in your age group, of course. But don't start wearing all this intense makeup. Be naturally beautiful. And beware of strange hairdos."

Hair, of course, must be very, very clean. Most models wash their hair every other day to keep it clean and fresh but manageable. "Some hair," says model Sarah Duffey, "only works well if it's slightly dirty. So those girls wash their hair the day before a job, not that morning. I wash my hair every day but every two days is probably better for most hair."

Sarah doesn't bother with expensive haircuts since her hair is cut in a straight, blunt cut. Often, her father cuts it for her. Though she believes she has learned a lot about her appearance since she started modeling, she thinks the important thing is to experiment on your own to see what's right for your particular type. "I've been to a lot of classes on makeup and I've learned a lot. Before, I just sort of threw my eye makeup on, and now I do it carefully. But I don't care what anyone says, it all comes down to doing it your own way."

Lynea Forseth's soft blonde hair was cut by professionals when she entered the modeling business. "I used to have longer hair," she says. "I could put it back in a braid and whatever. But Ford sent me to a hairdresser here in New York. They did what they thought was best."

Now Lynea has a layered cut that is shoulder-length. She has it cut every two months, and the rest of the time she handles it herself. Because her hair is fine and tends to be dry, she conditions the ends every other time she washes it. She never uses a blow dryer on her hair but lets it dry naturally or uses a heat lamp. As it dries, she runs her fingers through it to get the basic part and to untangle it. Combing or brushing while her hair is wet isn't a good idea, Lynea believes. "It prevents damage and gives my hair height just to finger-comb it," she says. "When it's dry, I curl it a bit."

Lynea's honey-blonde hair color is natural, though it is very reactive to the sun and is lighter in the summer than in the winter. Very few teenage models change the color of their hair with dyes or bleaches. Since the look they want is natural, they stick with their own hair color. "Once in a while," says Louise Roberts of Prestige, "we'll advise a girl to lighten her hair a bit by having sun streaks put in it. Just highlights."

It is part of Louise's work to teach her models how to handle their makeup and grooming. While most of the time models have makeup applied by a stylist when they are working on a job, they must apply their own makeup for go-sees and street wear. Louise believes, "It is part of the job for a model to know how to apply her own makeup. We bring in stylists and give them that as a seminar. We also teach them how to handle their hair. We give them simple styles such as the ponytail and twist to use in emergencies."

If you haven't got an agency to teach you makeup modeling tricks, how can you learn? Most models agree that experimentation is the best way to learn about your individual beauty style. Black model Tracey Ross says she's learned little about makeup and grooming since she came into the business because she had studied so hard before she broke in. "I went to the library and checked out every book I could on the subject of modeling. By the way, I never buy expensive brand names for my grooming. I use the most inexpensive, the most natural products I can find."

Several models suggested that large department stores have cosmetic salespeople who will make up your face to show you how to use their products. "Take advantage of every opportunity," one model suggested, "but don't buy the expensive cosmetics. You can do as well in the dime store."

Spending money for creams and cosmetics that promise instant beauty is a waste of money, most models agree. "I never buy those expensive facials," Tracey Ross says. "I use oatmeal or egg whites. If I have a pimple, I use baking soda and water to make a paste. Overnight, the pimple is gone."

Lynea Forseth, whose light-colored skin could be dry, says she really takes care of herself to prepare herself for her later years. "I use a moisturizer to prevent wrinkles. That and sleep and a well-balanced diet are really important."

One of the best ways to prevent wrinkling in later years is to avoid heavy tanning when you are young. Exposure to the sun should be gradual and you should never get sunburned. While light suntans are attractive, experts agree that deep tanning is bad for your skin.

Styles in makeup and hair change rapidly. For that reason, it is important to watch the fashions in teen magazines and try and keep track of what is current.

95

"Right now," Louise Roberts says, "short hair is very in. Two years ago, everyone wanted long, full hair."

While you must adjust to styles, you must also be aware of your own individual beauty type. In general, short hair is better on brunettes than blondes. "Long, straight hair only works for some," says Louise Roberts. "For most models, we want layered hair with fullness. It is more versatile." Louise adds this tip: "If you want your hair to look really full, bend forward and brush it. Then when you brush or comb it into place, it will retain most of that extra fullness."

Teased hair, tightly pulled-back hair, and extra-fancy hairstyles will make you look old-fashioned. So will getting too dressed up for job interviews. Most teen models wear pants and casual tops for go-sees. Though they are very clean and meticulously groomed, the general look is young and casual.

"We help our models pick out three cute outfits," says Louise Roberts of Prestige. "Pedal pushers, skirts, or slacks — but cute and casual."

Tracey Ross was wearing black slacks and a black sweater with low-heeled black pumps as she talked about dress. Around her neck was a simple strand of pearls. "I don't always dress up like this for go-sees," she says, "but I always try to look nice. I see girls who are wearing clothes that are not neat. They're sort of slouchy. They seem to think that is cool, but I was taught better than that. While it's true that nobody is interested in anything but your face, I try to look professional when I go on an interview for a job."

Some top models do seem to make a point of looking very sloppy as they appear for work, but that attitude and look are on their way out, according to

Eileen Ford of Ford Models Inc. She was quoted in *Time* magazine as saying that the sixties were "freaky" and the seventies were "slovenly," but in the eighties we're moving toward a "classic" look. A beginner should dress casually but as neatly and carefully as possible. Imitating the sloppy or slovenly look could make you look old-fashioned or just plain silly.

Dressing simply is nearly always a good idea. Typical of this simple dress are the clothes that top model Belinda Johnson of Wilhelmina wore on a go-see: blue corduroy slacks and a light blue sweater with tennis shoes. However, her honey-blonde hair was perfectly washed and arranged in a marvelous tumble of curls. Though not heavily made up, she'd obviously put a lot of thought and care into her appearance.

Lynea Forseth was wearing a checked blazer and a navy T-shirt with jodhpurs and penny loafers as she talked about the kind of dress she used for job interviews. "For TV, I wear T-shirts and Levi's because they want that young, all-American look," she said. "But for go-sees, I can express myself and I love it. In my high school, you basically wear jeans and T-shirts, but in New York City, I can be my own person. I wear the clothes I really like to go-sees and it seems to work out well."

Most models dress inconspicuously, avoiding ruffles, fancy jewelry, and high-fashion clothing because they want the photographers to see them, not the costumes they are wearing. They usually choose clothes that will go well with flat shoes because they do so much walking as they go from studio to studio.

If the job requires high heels, they may wear their running shoes to work and carry the heels in their tote bags.

Those tote bags contain a number of useful items for the model's trade. Extra shoes, makeup, nail polish, battery-operated curling iron, extra bra, panty hose, body stocking, and model assignment books are standard items. In addition, a model may carry her homework assignment or a book, an extra blouse or T-shirt, running shoes and other sports equipment, or even a fancy dress to go out on a date after the assignment.

The tote bag is a trademark of the working model and can be used for many different purposes; it contains many items for emergency repair. It serves as a combination notebook, briefcase, purse, and suitcase. It may be made of canvas, plastic, or soft leather but it must be large and lightweight. More and more girls are using gym bags as their tote bags. As long as it is useful, it is in style.

Models learn to pack their tote bags to respond to emergencies and they learn to pack for travel just as practically. Since successful fashion models often must go outside of photographers' studios for location shots, they must know how to pack quickly and simply. Sometimes location shots will be only a short train ride away but other times, they will be flights to fantastic places the models might never see otherwise.

You heard that Tracey Ross spent a week in Hawaii modeling clothes for *Woman's Day* magazine. Another "Tracy," Tracy Fitzpatrick, was featured in a *Seventeen* magazine story about her location work on the fabulous island of Aruba. Since most fashion shots are taken six months in advance, the summer features are often taken at tropical beaches in January or February. Tracy goes on three or four location trips a year and this time, her sister Tara was along.

Tracy is an expert at packing for location work, and all the clothes she took with her fit into one duffel bag. The list, as it appeared in *Seventeen* magazine, included:

A layered outfit for traveling in: jean jacket, T-shirt, sweat shirt, jeans, and boots.

Three white T-shirts: a top, a nightshirt, a beach coverup.

Three tank tops to wear with shorts or a skirt.

Three pairs of shorts: one dressy, two for play.

Two sundresses: one for comfort, one to dress up in.

One pair of dressy pants.

One all-purpose skirt.

One white sweater.

One swimsuit.

Shoes: one casual, comfy pair. One dressier pair. Sneakers, if planning sports activities.

Tracy and other models have learned to carry small amounts of makeup and lotions while on a trip. Often, you can save the sample sizes of cosmetics that you get when you buy large sizes. These work well for trips. If you don't have these sample tubes, you can buy plastic bottles in the dime store and pour small amounts of your makeup and lotions into them. Packing your liquids in plastic bottles inside plastic bags prevents spillage and breaking.

Traveling is more fun if your luggage is lightweight and practical. That means taking your most wrinkle-free and washable clothing. Often, if you select the easy-care fabrics, you can pack them into your duffel bag after you have rolled them tightly. When you get to the hotel room, unroll your dresses and separates and hang them on hangers. The wrinkles should hang out quickly.

Learning to select the proper clothing and wearing the right makeup and hairstyles are important parts of being a model. However, no amount of makeup or grooming knowledge will cover up poor health habits. Cleanliness, diet, and exercise are still the foundation stones of a modeling career. Once you have those basics down, you can learn some tricks of the trade that will help you look, act, and think like a successful model.

SPECIAL TIPS

HAIR TRICKS
For greater shine, try conditioning the ends of your hair every other time you wash it, as Lynea Forseth does. If your hair still seems dull, check your diet. Are you getting enough protein and vitamins A and B? Eggs, milk, and cheese supply these nutrients.

For greater body, try rinsing your hair in a beaten egg or stale beer once in a while as Donna Denton does. Leave the rinse on for ten minutes and wash it out.

For the perfect style, experiment a lot. Pull your hair up high, parting it in different ways and brushing it out until it is very full. You may want to have a friend take your picture with different hair silhouettes before you decide on a permanent cut. Remember Sarah Duffey's advice: "You have to find what's just right for you. Experiment until you know."

To change your face shape, your hairstyle is a great help. If your face is long, don't wear your hair pulled back or piled on top of your head. Try bangs and a classic pageboy. If your face is round, you will want an uneven side part like Lynea Forseth uses.

For greater versatility, remember Louise Roberts' advice. A shoulder-length layered cut will give you the most freedom to change hairstyles.

For dandruff, try massaging your hair every night before you go to bed. In the morning, give your hair an active brushing with a sparkling clean brush. This will loosen the dandruff, stimulate your scalp, and help your circulation. If the dandruff persists, check with your doctor — it may be a simple skin problem that he or she can cure.

For the cleanest hair, wash your combs and brushes every time you wash your hair. You can use your shampoo and then rinse them in water and a few drops of ammonia.

FIGURE TRICKS

To look taller, wear clothing of one color and never wear very, very high heels. It only calls attention to your lack of height. Remember that good posture makes you look taller.

To look shorter is almost never a good idea in the modeling game. Some models are over six feet tall these days. If you feel tall, walk proudly and keep your posture perfect. Take a yoga class to make yourself more graceful and less self-conscious, and every day, remind yourself that the most beautiful women in the world are tall.

To look slimmer, try wearing clothing of one dark color while you are dieting down to your ideal weight. Try scarves, jewelry, and pretty collars to draw attention to your face. Never, never wear clothes that are too tight for you.

To look heavier, you can wear clothes of different colors, wide shoulders and full, dramatic clothing. A diet that includes healthy foods like milk and whole grain cereals may help you put on weight in the right places.

SKIN TRICKS

For pimples or blemishes, try the baking soda and water paste that Tracey Ross recommends. It will dry up the pimple. Warning — never touch your face with unclean hands. Never squeeze pimples or blackheads. You might get an infection.

For blackheads, try a facial of oatmeal and water. The grainy texture may help you clean your face thoroughly. If you have a serious problem with blackheads, try washing and rinsing your face several times a day.

For acne, your best bet is to see a dermatologist and follow his or her advice to the letter. Many teens have acne, but these days few have permanent damage, especially if it is treated early.

For a refreshing facial, try a yogurt mask as Tracey Ross does for a quick, refreshing skin toner. Or if you feel in the need of a deep-cleansing facial, copy her recipe for oatmeal and egg whites. Beat two egg whites till frothy. Add a quarter cup of oatmeal and apply to your face. When it hardens, rinse off with cool water. It's inexpensive, effective, and all natural! *To protect your face*, use a moisturizer under your makeup and before you go to bed, as Lynea Forseth does. It is never too early to start taking care of your skin. And beware of the sun! Studies have shown that the biggest cause of wrinkling when you are older is sun when you are young.

HAND AND FOOT TRICKS

For a great manicure that will last and last, use a base coat of clear polish, two coats of color, and a top coat of clear. Then keep it shiny by adding a coat of color every third day.

For healthy cuticles, each time you wash your hands or feet, use your towel to push the cuticles back. A little cream will help do the job right.

For the right nail color, choose a light color that will harmonize with your clothing. Or use clear gloss or a pale pink tint. Never wear strange colors like green or purple. You are striving for a young, natural look.

Shape your nails in a short, blunt style if you want a natural, sporty look like Mary Beth Hoey has. Or if you have long, shapely nails like Tracey Ross, keep them perfectly manicured all the time. Never go on a go-see with chipped nail polish!

To stop biting your nails, start giving yourself wonderful manicures every two or three days. Never mind if you have no nails to paint! Use creams and lotions, clear polish, and do the job as well as you can. Pamper yourself and your soon-to-be-pretty hands.

For pedicures, cut your toenails straight across to avoid hangnails or ingrown toenails. Push back the cuticles and polish your toes just like you do your hands. Cream and an emery board or pumice stone will help with rough spots on your feet. Remember that keeping your feet pretty may pay off in modeling jobs.

For working in high heels, you will need some practice in order to walk naturally. Spend an hour a day in heels just to get the feel of it.

For dancing in heels, model Eśme Marshall says be sure and wear flats in the daytime. Switching shoes is an old trick for models and other workers who have to be on their feet all day long. Make sure the shoes have different heel heights to give your legs and ankles a break.

For tired feet, try soaking them in hot water before you give yourself a pedicure. Don't forget to massage them with cream as the first step toward prettier feet.

For softer, smoother feet, try putting cream on them before you go to bed as model P. J. Shaffer does. She covers her feet with cotton socks to keep the sheets from getting stained and keep the cream working.

MAKEUP TRICKS

For a perfect foundation, select a light creamy liquid that covers easily. Make sure the color is just slightly darker than your own coloring. Remember that Mary Beth Hoey advises: "The look is natural."

For a natural look, blend the foundation softly into your hairline and down your neck. Use a sponge to apply the makeup and soften the lines where the makeup ends.

For a beautiful mouth, remember that styles in lip

color change but the best bet is not to be too extreme. Teen models like Lynea Forseth prefer light pinks and soft roses in color.

To make your mouth look fuller, try covering your lips with foundation base and then extending your lip lines a bit, using a lipstick brush for careful work. Remember that extreme makeup is always wrong for the teen model.

For beautiful eyes, try using a little Vaseline on your eyelids to give them a glow without making them look made up. If you use eye shadow, make sure it is very light and well blended.

For longer lashes, powder your lids lightly, then apply a light coat of mascara. It is better to use two light coats of mascara than to apply one heavy one, as model Tracey Ross knows.

For brighter cheeks, suck in your cheeks to find your cheekbones. Then use light blusher, following the contour of the bones. Never make little round spots and don't bring the blusher into the cheek area.

These are just a few of the tricks that models learn about makeup and grooming. You will find many others by reading magazines and books about modeling, but remember that no matter how skillfully you apply makeup or fix your hair, you will need a foundation of good health. Diet and exercise are the real keys to the model's good looks.

WILDFIRE®

Move from one breathtaking romance to another with the #1
Teen Romance line in the country!

NEW WILDFIRES! $1.95 each

- ☐ MU32539-6 **BLIND DATE** Priscilla Maynard
- ☐ MU32541-8 **NO BOYS?** McClure Jones
- ☐ MU32538-8 **SPRING LOVE** Jennifer Sarasin
- ☐ MU31930-2 **THAT OTHER GIRL** Conrad Nowels

BEST-SELLING WILDFIRES! $1.95 each

- ☐ MU31981-7 **NANCY AND NICK** Caroline B. Cooney
- ☐ MU32313-X **SECOND BEST** Helen Cavanagh
- ☐ MU31849-7 **YOURS TRULY, LOVE, JANIE** Ann Reit
- ☐ MU31566-8 **DREAMS CAN COME TRUE** Jane Claypool Miner
- ☐ MU32369-5 **HOMECOMING QUEEN** Winifred Madison
- ☐ MU31261-8 **I'M CHRISTY** Maud Johnson
- ☐ MU30324-4 **I'VE GOT A CRUSH ON YOU** Carol Stanley
- ☐ MU32361-X **THE SEARCHING HEART** Barbara Steiner
- ☐ MU31710-5 **TOO YOUNG TO KNOW** Elisabeth Ogilvie
- ☐ MU32430-6 **WRITE EVERY DAY** Janet Quin-Harkin
- ☐ MU30956-0 **THE BEST OF FRIENDS** Jill Ross Klevin

📖 **Scholastic Inc.,**
P.O. Box 7502, 2932 E. McCarty Street, Jefferson City, MO 65102

Please send me the books I have checked above. I am enclosing $_____
(please add $1.00 to cover shipping and handling). Send check or money order—
no cash or C.O.D.'s please.

Name _____

Address_____

City_____ State/Zip_____

Please allow four to six weeks for delivery.   9/83